Alaska's Deadly Triangle

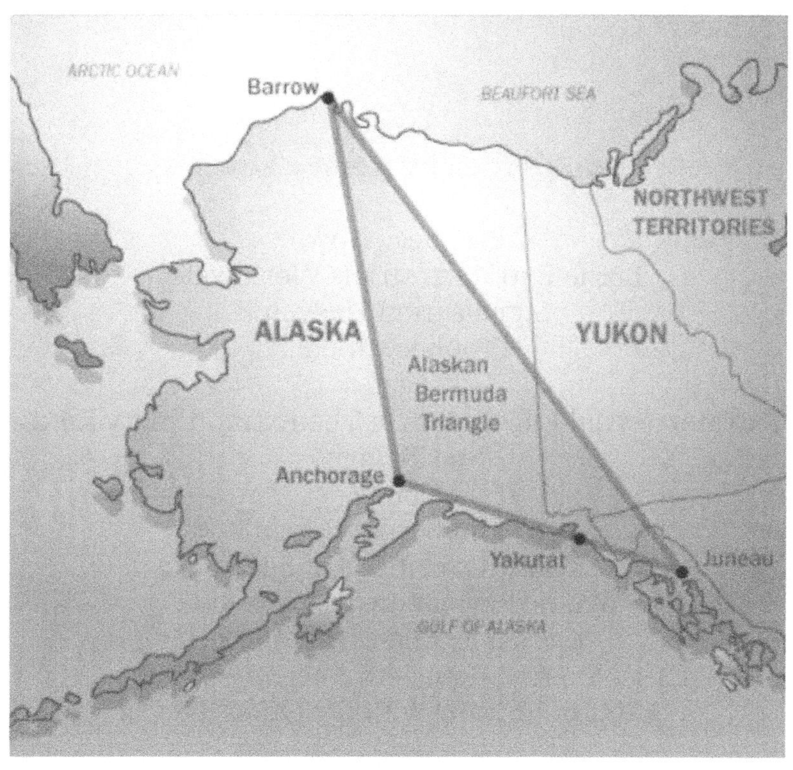

Book Titles by Betsey Lewis

Prophecy Now
Lizzie Extraterrestrials Worldwide
Signals from Heaven
Prophecy 2022
Stargates
Extraterrestrial Encounters of The Extraordinary Kind
Star Beings
Déjà vu
Ancient Serpent Gods
Mystic Revelations of Seven
Mystic Revelations of Thirteen
Baffled by Their Brilliance
Earth Energy: Return to Ancient Wisdom
Communicating with the Other Side

Children's Spiritual Books

Alexander Phoenix
The Story of Rainbow Eyes
A Worm Named Sherm

Alaska's Deadly Triangle

Betsey Lewis

Alaska's Deadly Triangle

ISBN: 979-8373423892

Cover design by Betsey Lewis

"Only the unknown frightens men. But once a man has faced the unknown, that terror becomes the known." – Antoine de Saint-Exupéry, French writer, poet, journalist and pioneering aviator.

CONTENTS

CHAPTER ONE

Alaska's Missing

There is a Triangle in Alaska one hundred times deadlier than the Bermuda Triangle off the coast of Florida where people disappear. Alaska's Deadly Triangle covers an area of untouched wilderness where anomalies are the norm, and where people simply vanish at a high rate. The Alaska Triangle connects the state's largest city of Anchorage in the south, to Juneau in the southeast panhandle, to Barrow, a small town on the state's north coast.

Alaska is the last great wilderness in the United States. Civilization has only encroached on about 160,000 acres of its 365 million acres. The State is a place of mostly uncharted remote areas where thousands of people have simply vanished without a trace.

Alaska is also a hotbed for UFO sightings, abductions, and

extraterrestrial encounters, Bigfoot sightings, a mysterious Dark Pyramid hidden inside a mountain that is believed to be millions of years old, and the existence of a huge lake monster.

Why would extraterrestrials be drawn to America's last frontier? It would be easy to hide in remote mountainous areas that are seldom explored. Alaska's population as of 2022 was only 733,683, approximately the same population as Seattle, Washington.

More than 16,000 people, including airplane passengers, hikers, locals, and tourists have disappeared within the infamous Alaska Triangle since 1988. The rate per 1,000 people is more than twice the national missing persons average, and the rate of people who are never found is even higher. Something deadly mysterious is going on there than getting lost in the wilderness.

Everything from extreme weather, geomagnetic anomalies, alien abductions, and energy laser experiments to government involvement, has been suggested.

Alaska is huge and the forested areas are dense. People have gotten lost in a snowstorm year-round, people fall and get stuck, and animals attack them, but something more, perhaps even more sinister is lurking in the tundra. Another far-out theory suggests that wormholes or portals exist in Alaska and people disappear into those portals/stargates and are transported to other places in the Universe, into the past, or even into the future.

The Triangle encompasses the state's largest city of Anchorage in the south to Juneau in the southeast panhandle. The Triangle became news in October 1972, when a small, private plane carrying U.S. House Majority Leader Hale Boggs, Alaska's Congressman Nick Begich, an aide named Russel Brown, and their bush pilot Don Jonz vanished without a trace while flying from Anchorage to Juneau. For over a month, 50 civilian planes and 40 military aircraft, and dozens of boats, combed the area consisting of 32,000 square miles and came up empty. No trace of the plane, the men, or any debris or wreckage were ever located.

In the months following Boggs' disappearance, Alaskan residents and tourists have vanished without a trace. Yearly,

500 to 2,000 people go missing in Alaska, never to be seen again. More than 16,000 human souls—airplane passengers, hikers, locals, and tourists, have vanished in the triangle area since 1988. Authorities conduct extensive searches but usually come up empty. Disappearances are blamed on the weather, UFOs, aliens, Big Foot, swirling vortexes, and evil shape-shifting demons of Tlingit Indian legends called *Kushtaka.*

Authorities and researchers believe the most common explanation for missing people includes the dangerous wilderness, forests, craggy mountain peaks, glaciers, hidden caves, and deep crevasses. A human can vanish in the snow-covered mountains, hiding them completely. There are wild animals such as grizzly, black bears, polar bears, wolves, wolverines, and moose. The Alaskan weather is known to change from mild to extreme within minutes. Avalanches and earthquakes might also contribute to missing people.

Alaska has 33,000 miles of coastline, more than three million lakes, lots of wildlife, and severe winters that blanket vast areas of the state in snow and ice. These conditions provide a more logical explanation for missing people, but some stories defy explanations.

But many investigators and ufologists believe an energy vortex or vortexes exist in the triangle. The energy spirals clockwise or counterclockwise, creating negative and positive polarities. Some theories suggest that stargates or vortexes connect alien beings to dimensional planes or into a past or future timeline.

Electronic readings taken in Alaska have shown large concentrations of magnetic anomalies, some of which have disrupted compasses to the point that they are as much as 30° degrees off. Magnetic anomalies have been found in the Bermuda Triangle off the coast of Florida and Japan's Devil Sea. It has been theorized that magnetic anomalies in the Bermuda Triangle and Japan's Devil Sea cause hallucinations, disorientation, and dizziness.

On July 9, 1947, three teenage Anchorage girls, Judy Kerr, Vicky Novack, and Nancy Green, claimed to see a white "disc-shaped object" above the Elmendorf Air Force base. The object streaked across the sky and disappeared to the south according to the girls and it traveled at "great speed and was moving faster than ordinary planes." The girls also claimed that it was smaller than any fighter plane and not a weather balloon, which they were familiar with since they were daughters of U.S. servicemen who liked to pass the time watching the base flight operations.

The three Anchorage girls made the first documented UFO sighting in Anchorage history. The girls promptly reported their sighting to the anchorage daily times. Before that week, there had been zero references to "flying saucers" or "flying discs" printed in the local newspapers, covering the previous 32 years of anchorage's existence. On July 7, the daily times ran its first article on the UFO craze, just two days before the three girls claimed to see something over Elmendorf. on July 8, the daily times published the first local coverage of the developing story out of Roswell, fueled by the original army press release that described the weather balloon as a "flying disc." the article also noted, "none have been reported in Alaska, yet."

Then, the very next day, three teenagers just happened to see a UFO.

No one else from either the army, air force, or Merrill Field saw the UFOs. Lee Teague, special agent in charge of the anchorage FBI office, stated, "we haven't heard a single report of any persons seeing a flying disc in anchorage, or even Alaska."

As it happened across the nation, once one person made a UFO sighting, more reports followed. a railroad foreman claimed to have seen a flying saucer in Healy six weeks prior but had declined to report it "for fear of being laughed at."

In January 1950, retired fisherman Jorgen Mortenson said he saw a flying saucer outside his cabin at Jamestown Bay. Mortenson stated, "I am positively not mistaken. I saw it but did not mention it as I thought people would think me a little off." Over a week that October, there were seven UFO sightings in Sitka. on November 30, 1950, a "brilliant blue-white" object, almost certainly a meteor, flashed across the sky with sightings from Fairbanks to Kodiak. in early

November 1952, two men reported a "strange light bouncing up and down in the sky" over Anchorage.

In 1953, six women claimed to have watched a flying saucer passing back and forth over Eklutna for two hours. The foto shop on Fourth Avenue got in on the fun and offered a $200 reward in 1947, roughly $2,700 in 2022 dollars, for "one authentic flying disc or flying saucer."

They wanted an actual flying saucer, not a photograph of one as their announcement stated, "we want one so that we can take a picture of to add to our large collection. So just carry, haul, or fly one up to the door and collect your reward."

Flying saucers have been embedded in American popular culture, including in Alaska. By December 1947, Anchorage shops had the new record from the Buchanan brothers, "those flying saucers." There were flying disc dances in anchorage and a flying saucer delivery service in Fairbanks. Multiple boats in Alaska were named the flying saucer, including a hydroplane that raced at lake Wasilla. This wave of interest began with the first UFO movie made in 1950 titled, *The Flying Saucer*.

In 2016, Garrett Augustine, a security officer, was leaving work at three in the morning and suddenly watched one huge orb appear in the sky. As he watched in disbelief, the orb split into three orbs and then vanished.

In 2005, mountain climber Darrin Markam was descending from a successful climb near the infamous Mount Hayes as he worked his way to base camp. That's when the rocks around him began to glow bright green, and then he looked up to see an egg-shaped orb glowing green. In the dark, Darrin descended to base camp to check on his friend Sidney Yanovic, but when he reached their camp there was no sign of his friend. Darrin found it extremely strange that he would leave his equipment. Not even footprints were in the snow. To this day, no one knows what happened to Sidney Yanovic.

On January 26, 1950, the Douglas C-54 Skymaster 42-72469 disappeared en route from Alaska to Montana, carrying forty-four people. The aircraft made its last radio contact two hours into its eight-hour flight. Search and rescue of this plane consisted of 85 American and Canadian planes, in addition to 7,000 personnel combing 350,000 square miles of the Northwest. Nothing was ever found of the Douglas C-54 Skymaster and the 44 people. It was one of the largest groups of American Military personnel to ever go missing.

In 2003, a squadron of UFOs was witnessed by Charles Gaines outside of Fairbanks. It started with three or four orbs and grew in number. Some speed-up and make incredible turns, impossible for any conventional airplane. He stated it was like watching an “armada” (fleet) in the sky.

Alaska’s State MUFON (Mutual UFO Network) Director, Jesse Desmond researched a 1978 story about a group of hikers who camped out in the wilderness of Alaska and watched a craft land not far from them. The next morning, they decided to search for the UFO that appeared to land the night before. Instead of finding an alien craft, they were sickened by what they discovered. There were dead carcasses of bear, moose, caribou, and a 15’ foot whale strewn around the area—all mutilated in the middle of the forest, miles from the coast.

The History Channel’s *Missing in Alaska* series debuted in 2015 with investigators Tommy Joseph, Jax Atwell, and Ken Gerhard. Their investigated stories are truly baffling. Such as the village that vanished in 1930. A newspaper in Manitoba reported on a small Inuit village beside Lake Angikuni that had mysteriously vanished. The village had always welcomed fur trappers who passed by. But that year, Joe Labelle, a fur trapper, known by the village, found the entire village had vanished.

Labelle found unfinished shirts with needles in them and food hanging over fire pits, indicating the villagers suddenly left. What disturbed him more was that seven sled dogs died from starvation and a grave had been dug up. Labelle knew an animal could not have done that because of stones circling the grave were undisturbed. He reported his findings to the Royal Canadian Mounted Police who searched for the missing villagers, but not one person was ever found.

The *Missing in Alaska* team journeyed to Mount Hayes to investigate claims an alien underground base exists there. They brought Wilbur Allen, an alien abductee and remote viewer, who said, "I feel them around the area."

Allen has been abducted by aliens beginning at the age of five when five small gray beings in silver suits entered his bedroom and telepathically talked to him and then he blacked out.

The team discovered after tethering up to get to base camp that the ground has shifted from the previous night. While there in the dark, the team and Wilbur heard a rumble and spotted a white orb over Mount Hayes and wondered if it was a plane. But that was soon ruled out because the object traveled slowly and then sped up, vanishing into the stars.

Their number 3 trail camera captured the UFO and its unconventional moves to hover like a helicopter, and also reverse instantly unlike any known aircraft. The object had a ramping up speed from a standstill and based on its relativity to the Mountain, the team calculated its speed of just over Mach 1 or 761 miles per hour.

The next day, they sent up a drone to survey the area and found what looked like a snow circle only oval-shaped, measuring 15.5' feet by 22' feet exactly. The Geiger counter indicated radiation fluctuation through the snow. They took two samples of the snow and left, fearful of dangerous radiation levels in the area.

Samples of the snow were sent to Jim Anderson at the University of Alaska's Earth Sciences Laboratory in Fairbanks, north of Mount Hayes. The first sample was like water—nothing extraordinary about it. But the second sample was unexpected. The sample contained large amounts of tungsten, which either came from outer space or deep underground. It tested out at 50 parts per million of Tungsten. In other words, 0.1 parts per million are normal, making the sample 500 times stronger. Tungsten is not radioactive and was not an explanation for the increase in radiation near the peculiar oval in the snow.

Tungsten, or Wolfram, is a chemical element with the symbol "*W*" and the atomic number 74. Tungsten is a rare metal found naturally on Earth almost exclusively as a compound with other elements. It's never pure like the samples taken near Mount Hayes. Current uses are in electrodes, heat elements, field emitters, filaments in light bulbs, and cathode-ray tubes. Tungsten is also the strongest metal on Earth.

What could aliens be using tungsten metal for? Their spacecraft perhaps?

CHAPTER TWO

Stargates and Holographic Inserts

Besides UFOs or USOs (unidentified submerged objects) diving into the world's oceans, there are stories and legends of deep underground alien bases throughout the world where humans are taken for genetic experiments. Theories suggest some of the areas known for UFO activity and mysterious disappearances of people, ships, and aircraft are known to be portals or stargates to other dimensions. Stories include well-known alien abductees who were taken to undersea cities or bases.

Portals or stargates are hidden entrances to other dimensions or worlds and entrances to places on Earth. Planets also have doors through which can be entered. Portals are composed of the corridors of time. When you enter a planet, how can you be assured which era you will end up in when all time is simultaneous? When you leave a planetary sphere and go into space, once you traverse certain belts of consciousness you must find the proper portal to come back into the planet in the precise time or corridor of time that you are looking for. A planet might appear devoid of life on the outside, but once it is accessed through a portal, life is abundant there.

There are portals on the South American continent, the North American continent, Asia, China, and all over the entire globe. Many extraterrestrials access the portals to travel great distances in the Universe in a short time. Native Americans created spinning spirals in rock throughout the West, which might have been their knowledge of portals. The spiral was derived from Native Americans as the symbol for eternity or the path of our existence on Earth. Spiral etchings can be found in ancient caves and etched in stone worldwide.

Tibet and the Middle East are both dimensional doorways or entryways onto the planet for certain energies. The Middle East is a hot spot for violence and war and that's because it is a portal where many dimensions meet and where entities from other dimensions can come onto this planet. In the last forty or fifty thousand years, many civilizations have surfaced, and many religious dramas have started in the Middle East. Because of the vortex, holographic inserts are easier to produce in that area, just like movies are easier to produce in California.

You may find this hard to believe, but even the Christed One's life was only a version of this entity's life which was molded and designed in a holograph entertainment movie, which was then inserted and played out as if it were real. Many human dramas were holograph inserts to control you. The purpose of holographic inserts or dramas have been used through the Middle East portal to upset the minds and beliefs of the human who live there. Since the region of the world is in the midst of a crisis, like other areas of the world, it is a prime candidate for holographic inserts and also prime for a belief system to be altered in our chaotic world.

Be aware of how these dramas make you feel—anger, hate, upset, and how that vibrational energy encompasses the planet.

Scientists have speculated for years that wormholes exist throughout the universe, a hypothetical structure connecting disparate points in spacetime, and is based on a special solution of the Einstein field equations. A wormhole can be visualized as a tunnel with two ends at separate points in spacetime.

Several places around the world are known to be energetic hotspots from ancient megalith stone structures to Ley Lines that are alleged to produce hyper-dimensional gateways. Some of these renowned places exist at Mt. Shasta in Northern California, Alaska, Sedona, Arizona, the Skinwalker Ranch in southeastern Utah, the San Luis Valley in southern Colorado, the Bermuda Triangle off the coast of Florida, and a prime portal in the Middle East, where they have a major base underground. Other stargates or portals exist in Mexico/Central America, Mount Fuji, Easter Island, Lake Titicaca, Sinai, Tibet, Uluru in Australia, Peru, and the Nazca Lines. Ancient crystal skulls found near these portal areas are believed to hold the resonance of the Earth's grid. For example, the Tibetan monks accessed the portals near their monasteries and temples in the Himalayas, learning of the evil plan to invade their country by the Chinese, and so they quickly hid many of their most sacred documents, treasures, and artifacts years before the invasion. China continues to seek this knowledge from the monks through torture.

While we don't exactly know how to open a portal to another dimension, there is evidence ETs understand how to access them. And now it seems science may be catching on to the possibility of portals. Typically, portal areas have some type of electromagnetic significance and are located near large deposits of quartz or other minerals with piezoelectric properties. So, it came as less of a surprise when NASA announced in 2012 that the University of Iowa's physicist Jack Scudder found hard evidence of portals created by the interaction between the Earth and the Sun's magnetospheres.

These portals are extremely volatile and unpredictable, opening and closing in a matter of an instant. But Scudder found markers, called x-points or electron diffusion regions, which allowed NASA probes to locate and study them. These energetic locales are considered sacrosanct because they represent areas where our inner temple—the mind can access higher states of consciousness, connecting with extradimensional entities or invoking out-of-body experiences. Whether these areas always represented dimensional portals for the mind, or a portal for the physical body is up for debate.

Graham Hancock wrote about native shamans traversing planes of consciousness using a psychedelic substance such as ayahuasca. Within this ecstatic state, shamans report meeting teachers and guides, who provide advice and wisdom for living within the everyday realm of our existence. But Hancock also says he believes it is worth considering that there may be something otherworldly to these portal areas; something beyond materialist comprehension.

One location that seems to fit this description is Puerta de Hayu Marca in Peru. Situated on a plateau just off the western banks of Lake Titicaca, Puerta de Hayu Marca translates to the Gate of the Gods. Reaching 23 feet in both height and width, Hayu Marca appears to be a doorway to nowhere carved into a rock face in a remote area known as the Valley of the Spirits or Stone Forest.

Hayu Marca rests on what is believed to be a Ley Line, and the famous Gate of the Sun at Tiwanaku also lies in nearby Bolivia, along with several other important Incan archaeological points. This huge mysterious door-like structure in the Hayu Marca Mountain region of Southern Peru near Lake Titicaca lies 35 kilometers from the city of Puno and is found in an area that has long been honored by local indigenous people as the "City of the Gods." Although no actual city has ever been discovered, the area is known as a Spirit Forest, or Stone Forest, made of strange rock formations that resemble buildings, people, and other artificial structures (Simulacrum).

Ley Lines are Mother Earth's energy points that connect worldwide. The Ley Lines are electrical currents that are like veins in the planet, and it is believed ancient humans accessed these energy points that coil around the planet. Ley Lines are known to crisscross around the globe, like latitudinal and longitudinal lines, which are dotted with monuments and natural landforms, and carry rivers of supernatural energy. Along these lines, at the places they intersect, there are pockets of concentrated energy, that can be harnessed by certain individuals.

The Indigenous Indians of the region have a legend that spoke of "a gateway to the lands of the Gods", and it said that long, long ago great heroes had gone to join their gods and passed through the gate for a glorious new life of immortality, and on rare occasions, those men returned for a short time with their gods to "inspect all the lands in the kingdom" through the gate.

Another legend tells of the time when the Spanish Conquistadors arrived in Peru and looted gold and precious stones from the Inca tribes. According to one of the legends, an Incan priest of the Temple of the Seven Rays named *Amaru Meru* (Aramu Muru) fled from his temple with a sacred golden disk known as "the key of the gods of the seven rays" and hid in the mountains of Hayu Marca. He eventually came upon the doorway which was being watched by shaman priests. He showed them the key to the gods and a ritual was performed with the conclusion of a magical occurrence initiated by the golden disk which opened the portal, and according to the legend, blue light did emanate from a tunnel inside.

The priest Amaru Meru handed the golden disk to the shaman and then passed through the portal "never to be seen again." Archeologists have observed a small hand-sized circular depression on the right-hand side of the small entranceway and have theorized that this is where a small disk could be placed and held by the rock.

Visitors to Peru's Hayu Marca have reported unusual energy fields there with some claiming they can feel pulsating energy from the rock when placing their hand in its center. Many who have reviewed the ancient site online also mention this feeling of elevated or intense energy there.

Lake Titicaca nearby was revered by the Incas and considered to be the birthplace of their civilization. It is also among the deepest lakes in the world, rumored to contain a lost city and a plethora of treasures looted by the Spanish. In 2000, the lost temple of Atahualpa was discovered deep below the lake, adding to the mysterious nature of this ancient culture. It has been noted that the structure superficially resembles the Gate of the Sun at Tiwanaku (Tiahuanaco). It is also said to be aligned by five other archaeological sites which together form an imaginary cross with straight lines crossing each other exactly at the point where the plateau and Lake Titicaca are located.

Planets also have doors through which you can enter portals composed of corridors of time. The Tibetans, until the 1950s, maintained an energy doorway. Over hundreds of years, they have acted as guardians and emissaries for those who ventured through. According to the same source, Tibetans have been working with extraterrestrials for eons.

The Maya and Aztecs hid their gold caches. They understood that Gold is part of what allows dimensional doorways to be opened. They anchor portals and bring about transmutations. The gold caches around the globe contain great secrets that are utilized to open stargates and anchor energy. There are huge veins and rivers of gold conducting frequencies throughout Earth that are an essential part of life. Gold is often found accompanied by quartz crystals, which are modern-day founding stones in all our communication devices.

Harvard psychiatrist John E. Mack (1929-2004) had a conversation with the Dalai Lama about aliens in 1994. Mack was well-versed in extra-terrestrials. Having already spent decades conducting research with hundreds of extraterrestrial experiencers and abductees in North America, he had built a career on trying to make sense of the alien abduction experience.

The Dalai Lama knows a thing or two about aliens as well. He explained to Mack and a small group that aliens were sentient beings in the universe. He also corroborated Mack's theory that these entities were making contact because they were disturbed by humans' destruction of the environment.

A few years later in 1999, Dr. Mack met with the Dalai Lama again in Dharamsala, India, as part of a symposium on world peace. During this visit, Mack recorded an interview about his interview with the Dalai Lama about aliens. According to Mack, for high-level Tibetan lamas like the Dalai Lama who "live at the level of "mystical formlessness," dramatic alien contact and abduction were unlikely.

Realized beings like the Dalai Lama had visitations and contact with "a vast array of entities and beings that are very real for them in the cosmos" and so they took for granted a contra-materialist, contra-Western worldview where "things can cross from the unseen world into the material world." It simply didn't make sense for them to have the kind of shattering, consciousness-expanding abduction experiences that were typical of Mack's more run-of-the-mill North American research subjects.

The Dalai Lama's level of consciousness is so advanced that it made encountering an alien consciousness unnecessary. Simplified—the Dalai Lama was already on the aliens' wavelength.

Utah's Skinwalker Ranch Portal

Since Brandon Fugal purchased the infamous Skinwalker Ranch in northeastern Utah in 2016 from Robert Bigelow, his scientific team has witnessed UAP (unidentified aerial phenomena) appear and suddenly vanish as if the orb or object entered a portal. Skinwalker Ranch is one of the strangest places where people have witnessed UFOs entering an opening in the Mesa, orbs flying around in an abandoned home or around the ranch, cattle mutilated or found dead, and fluctuations of radiation seeming targets at certain people on the Ranch.

CHAPTER THREE

Alaska's Deadly Triangle

Alaska's Triangle became news in October 1972, when a small, private plane carrying U.S. House Majority Leader Hale Boggs, Alaska's Congressman Nick Begich, an aide named Russel Brown, and their bush pilot Don Jonz vanished without a trace while flying from Anchorage to Juneau. For over a month, 50 civilian planes and 40 military aircraft, and dozens of boats, combed the area consisting of 32,000 square miles and came up empty. No trace of the plane, the men, or any debris or wreckage were ever located.

In the months following Boggs' disappearance, Alaskan residents and tourists have vanished without a trace. Yearly, 500 to 2,000 people go missing in Alaska, never to be seen again. More than 16,000 human souls—airplane passengers, hikers, locals, and tourists, have vanished in the triangle area since 1988. Authorities conduct extensive searches but usually come up empty. Disappearances are blamed on the weather, UFOs, aliens, Bigfoot, swirling vortexes, and the evil shape-shifting demons of Tlingit Indian legends called *Kushtaka*.

But authorities and researchers believe the most common explanation for missing people includes the dangerous wilderness, forests, craggy mountain peaks, glaciers, hidden caves, and deep crevasses. A human can vanish in the snow-covered mountains, hiding them completely. There are wild animals such as grizzly, black bears and polar bears, wolves, wolverines, and moose. The Alaskan weather is known to change from mild to extreme within minutes. Avalanches and earthquakes might also contribute to missing people.

Alaska has 33,000 miles of coastline, more than three million lakes, lots of wildlife, and severe winters that blanket vast areas of the state in snow and ice.

But many investigators and ufologists believe an energy vortex or vortexes exist in the triangle. The energy spirals clockwise or counterclockwise, creating negative and positive polarities. Some theories suggest that stargates or vortexes connect alien beings to dimensional planes or into past or future timelines.

Electronic readings taken in Alaska have shown large concentrations of magnetic anomalies, some of which have disrupted compasses to the point that they are as much as 30° degrees off. Magnetic anomalies have been found in the Bermuda Triangle off the coast of Florida and Japan's Devil Sea. The anomalies can cause hallucinations, disorientation, and dizziness. Of course, there are always logical explanations for disappearances, especially in Alaska, but there are cases that can't be easily dismissed as weather, wildlife, and environmental conditions. Strange UFO sightings are common in Alaska. In 2016, Garrett Augustine, a security officer, was leaving work at three in the morning and suddenly watched one huge orb appear in the sky. As he watched in disbelief, the orb split into three orbs and then vanished.

In 2005, mountain climber Darrin Markam was descending from a successful climb near the infamous Mount Hayes as he worked his way to base camp. That's when the rocks around him began to glow bright green, and then he looked up to see an egg-shaped orb glowing green. In the dark,

Darrin descended to base camp to check on his friend Sidney Yanovic, but when he reached their camp there was no sign of his friend. Darrin found it extremely strange that he would leave his equipment. Not even footprints were in the snow. To this day, no one knows what happened to Sidney Yanovic.

The Case of the Missing Douglas C-54

As mentioned earlier in the book, one of the more baffling disappearances took place on January 26, 1950, on a good weather day. The Douglas C-54 Skymaster 42-72469 aircraft disappeared on that day en route from Alaska to Montana, carrying forty-four people. The aircraft made its last radio contact two hours into its eight-hour flight. Search and rescue of this plane consisted of 85 American and Canadian planes, in addition to 7,000 personnel combing 350,000 square miles of the Northwest. Nothing was ever found of the Douglas C-54 Skymaster and the 44 people on board. It was one of the largest groups of American Military personnel to ever go missing.

The aircraft was part of the Second Strategic Support Squadron, Strategic Air Command out of Briggs Air Force Base, Texas.

In addition to its eight-man military crews, it was carrying 36 passengers including a civilian woman and her infant son. At first, the aircraft had made an initial attempt to depart, but was delayed several hours after reporting trouble with one of its four engines.

The aircraft was flying from Anchorage, Alaska to Great Falls, Montana; two hours after its eventual departure the pilot reported it was on course and had just passed over Snag, Yukon. The was the last transmission.

One hour after it failed to show up in Montana, *"Operation Mike"*, named for aircraft commander First Lt. Kyle L. McMichael, was launched, a search and rescue program combining as many as 85 American and Canadian planes, in addition to 7,000 personnel, searching 350,000 square miles of the Pacific Northwest. The search was aided by the fact soldiers and equipment had already been ferried north for the upcoming Exercise Sweetbriar, a joint Canada-US war games scenario.

However, the continuation of the operation confounded searchers, giving many false positive reports of smoke signals, strange, garbled communications and sightings of "survivors".

On January 30, a C-47 from the 57th Fighter Wing that had been participating in the search, stalled and crashed in the McClintock Mountains and its crew members were all injured, but there were no fatalities. Its pilot walked 13 km to the Alaska Highway and flagged down a truck to call in support for his 5-8 crewmates.

Later, (February 7 or February 16) a Royal Canadian Air Force C-47, *KJ-936*, crashed near Snag. Again, its four crew members sustained only light injuries. Later its wreckage would be temporarily mistaken for the missing C-54.

The operation was indefinitely suspended on February 14, as the search planes were needed to investigate the crash of a B-36 on February 13 that had been carrying, and dropped its Fat Man Type nuclear weapon.

It has been suggested that the plane was downed because someone special was on board even though the manifest never showed any name of the missing as special. Was it carrying a warhead? In 1950, tensions were high between Russia and the United States. Another theory is that Alaska is known for its strange electromagnetic properties that cause compasses to malfunction including instrument failure.

1950 also recorded UFOs stalking military planes before the Douglas incident. Radar had clocked the UFOs moving at 1,800 mph. No human aircraft could fly at those speeds during that time. It was noted that for some time faint radio signals were picked up and distorted voices were heard as if coming from the down plane, and then it stopped. The signals could not be traced. Ufologists theorize the Douglas vanished into a dimensional vortex or parallel world that exists only as a vibration away from our world.

Two Consolidated-Vultee B-36B Peacemaker long-range strategic bombers of the 436th Bombardment Squadron (Heavy), 7th Bombardment Wing (Heavy), Strategic Air

Command, departed Eielson Air Force Base (EIL), Fairbanks, Alaska, at 4:27 p.m., Alaska Standard Time (01:27 UTC), on a planned 24-hour nuclear strike training mission. B-36B-15-CF 44-92075 was under the command of Captain Harold Leslie Barry, United States Air Force. There was a total of seventeen men on board. Also on board was a Mark 4 nuclear bomb. Due to extreme cold and icing on the planes, the mission was scrubbed. The Air Force decided to jettison the atomic bomb into the Pacific Ocean.

The Aftermath of the Missing Douglas

On February 20, the search was officially canceled, and notifications were sent to next of kin informing them that the passengers were presumed dead. There were two contemporary reports of unidentified flying objects by officers stationed at Elmendorf AFB, the first a week before the disappearance, and the second two days after the disappearance. On April 19, Sgt. William Y. Harrell reported from the control tower that he had seen two UFOs hovering over a hangar emitting a green light, a report backed by other soldiers at the base. On January 28, Lt. Col. Lester F. Mathison reported seeing three orange cigar-shaped UFOs flying in tandem above the base. Both cases were investigated by the Alaskan Air Command, which ruled only that the objects were neither weather phenomena nor recognized aircraft. The latter incident has also been cataloged as happening on January 26, within hours of the C-54's last transmission.

In 2012, the descendants of the missing servicemen started a petition to the Federal government, through the We the People petition system, seeking to resurrect the search for their families' remains.

Squadron of UFOs over Fairbanks, Alaska

In 2003, a squadron of UFOs was witnessed by Charles Gaines outside of Fairbanks. It started with three or four orbs and grew in numbers. Some speed-up and make incredible turns, impossible for any conventional airplane. He stated it was like watching an "armada" (fleet) in the sky.

Alaska's State MUFON (Mutual UFO Network) Director, Jesse Desmond researched a 1978 story about a group of hikers who camped out in the wilderness of Alaska and watched a craft land not far from them. The next morning, they decided to search for the UFO that appeared to land the night before. Instead of finding an alien craft, they were sickened by what they discovered. There were dead carcasses of bears, moose, caribou, and a 15' foot whale strewn around the area—all mutilated in the middle of the forest, miles from the coast.

Military Reserve on Training Mission near Mt. Hayes

In 2015, Matt Schaefer was on a typical military reserve helicopter training exercise near Fort Greely, located near Mount Hayes. While in flight, without warning, the helicopter was hit by a jolt and followed within minutes by a second one. Outside the helicopter was a brilliant light hovering in the sky. It suddenly raced away, and Matt and his reserve officers returned to base without further incident.

Remote Viewer Patrick Price

For two decades, beginning in the 1960s, remote viewers were used in government and military experiments to see if certain target areas could be remotely viewed. Patrick Price was a remote viewer. He was a former Burbank, California police officer and former Scientologist who participated in several Cold War remote viewing experiments, including the U.S. government-sponsored projects SCANATE and the Stargate Project.

Price's involvement with the remote projects was an accident. He was introduced by fellow Scientologists Harold Puthoff and Ingo Swann near SRI International, an American nonprofit scientific research institute, located in Menlo Park, California.

Price claimed to be able to retrieve information into Soviet facilities by working with maps and photographs provided by the CIA. He is best known for his sketches of cranes and gantries which appeared to conform to CIA intelligence photographs. Because of Price's special remote viewing ability, the CIA at the time took his claims seriously.

Patrick Price

Price claimed ETs had established four underground bases and provided Harold Puthoff with vivid descriptions of their locations and functions. Puthoff directed the remote viewing program at SRI from 1972 to 1985 in which Price was involved. Puthoff eventually passed Price's remote viewing folder on to Captain F. Holmes "Skip" Atwater, founder of the U.S. Army's Remote Viewing Unit in the early 1980s, saying, "You might be interested in this." At that time, Price's information was viewed with protocols, and the results were not officially reported.

Those who knew Price believed him because he had a proven remote viewing track record and had no agenda. Price's report about the Mount Hayes base's primary purpose was to 'reinforce B.T.L. implants (an acronym for *Between the Lives)*, transport recruits and overall monitory function.' Captain F. Holmes "Skip" Atwater at the time was the founder of the U.S. Army's remote viewing unit.

The extraterrestrials described by Price were human in

appearance, but their heart, lungs, blood, and eyes were different. He reported that the sites were highly protected from discovery, mutually supportive, and well-advanced in science and technology. He also wrote they used 'thought transfer for motor control of humans.' "Actually, it's more of a maintenance and tech center," Price noted. "I see lots of spare equipment. Parts are welded in a vacuum area with a window area then parts are fused. A grayish-white powder is pasted on both parts and then fused."

In his viewing, Price had drawn the unit area—a tubular grid system for 'ionizing a layer of air.'

One day while he asked to view a secret Soviet site his attention was pulled away to Alaska's Mount Hayes. What he had remotely viewed was frightening—a secret alien underground base inside the mountain. He observed humanoids working with normal humans in military uniforms.

Mount Hayes is the highest mountain in the eastern Alaska Range. The climate there is subarctic with cold, snowy winters, and mild summers. Temperatures can drop below -20° C with a wind chill factor below -30° C. There are glaciers on its slopes which makes climbing Mount Hayes especially dangerous.

Price said that Mount Hayes is a weather and geological center and had cloaking technology to hide the base from the outside world. He described computer equipment and followed leads on an oscilloscope which led to a small box-like structure that contained a rotational antenna that sat on top of a mountain peak. The receiver seemed to be part of a detection system. If the underground base was discovered, personnel were deployed to make sure that there was a malfunction of U.S. and Soviet Space Projects in the area.

Atwater suggested that if a probe was launched over this part of Alaska, it might be interfered with in some way, to prevent detection of the Mount Hayes base. "It comes to mind that these 'people' (aliens) have infiltrated all government in sensitive positions, not to control government, but rather to be in positions of power to stop politically any activity that may produce a result that could cause discovery."

Price described and sketched much of what he was viewing—*triangular peak, inside domed, cavernous, tunnels, rough, natural, two persons outside, fossils, music box melody, remind me of Switzerland. The site appears to be a structure located within a mountain that has a triangular peak (Mount Hayes), there is a large lake at the base of this mountain which is surrounded by high rugged mountains or cliffs. It seems fairly impenetrable. There were two people walking around outside of the structure and two people inside the structure. One of the people inside the structure sat at a circular position which appeared to look similar to an organ because of the keys, buttons, and switches (the world "observing" comes to mind, and it appeared to be some sort of screen or monitor, but I could not make it out clearly.*

The Entity at the console appears to be human in form but lacks definitive facial features and seems friendly enough and invited me to observe his actions at the console.

For this session, I was completely blind as to what the target was. I was given only a set of coordinates (63° 37° 15" N, 146° 42' 55' W) and asked to describe the location. The coordinates given were the actual latitude/longitude of Mt. Hayes, Alaska.

Mount Hayes, Alaska has a triangular peak.

Price's Mount Hayes and description of an ET base seem like a fantasy, but when you connect the dots of missing people, UFO reports, and other anomalies and paranormal events in certain areas around the world, there just might be something to Price's remote viewing. Former CIA director

Stansfield Turner described Price in the Chicago Tribune, on August 13, 1977, as “A man who could see what was going on anywhere in the world through his psychic powers.’

Price died under mysterious circumstances on July 14, 1975, in Las Vegas, and those who knew him or investigated his story believed he was murdered because he knew too much about the extraterrestrials and the military working together like Phil Schneider who discussed openly what he witnessed as an engineer creating massive underground tunnels for the U.S. Military in 1979 at Dulce, New Mexico, where many died from the firefight between the military and the 7’ foot aliens. Schneider also died under mysterious circumstances on January 17, 1996.

Remoter viewer Lori Williams says the aliens at Mount Hayes are human-like and cunning, scientifically advanced, and doing experiments underground. What they are doing concerns Earth.

Strange human encounters on remote roads happen often in Alaska. One night Jerry Wilcox was returning home to an isolated area of northern Alaska after work when an odd noise startled him. He couldn’t believe a man was standing on the road in front of his car. He slammed on his brakes but as he was about to hit the man he vanished into thin air. He looked in the rearview mirror and could see him standing behind the car, a creepy black figure. A bright light engulfed his car as he got out as if commanded to do so. A craft hovered above him. Suddenly a wolf howled in the distance, snapping him out of his trance-like state. The UFO had already vanished in the night as Jerry drove home, bewildered. He was missing hours and couldn’t recall why.

An Alien, A Spacecraft, and an Alaskan Blizzard

During an interview with Dr. Ardy Sixkiller Clarke in 2014, I was shocked about the stories she heard by Native Americans and Alaskan Natives who have experienced countless alien encounters. This story is from Clarke’s book, *Encounters with Star People*.

This story happened to an Alaskan Native, half

Athabascan, and half Aleut, named Ross who came upon an alien in the middle of the road during a blizzard. True to the Alaskan code of honor, he invited the alien to join him in his vehicle for fear he would freeze in the 70° degree below zero night.

The year was not given in the story, but it was in February when a raging blizzard hit the area and he was snowbound in a motel. Winds were 50 mph with a wind chill that hovered 70° below zero. Ross was going to keep the roads clear, and that means driving 18-hour shifts. He headed out into the weather.

Usually, he and another driver met at Lucky Gil's, an inn with a bar and restaurant. Another driver named Bill claimed he witnessed a strange glow beyond Lucky Gil's. He asked if Ross had seen it. Back on the highway, Ross saw a disk sitting in the middle of the highway. It covered two full lanes, and it was round with bright orange lights around the bottom.

Suddenly, blinding white lights turned on and the craft moved upward and was gone. But it wasn't long before the blizzard cut visibility on the highway to nearly zero. When it was gone, there was darkness around him. Next, his engine died, and he didn't turn it off for fear it would never turn over again in the extreme temperature. He tried again, and the engine started. As his plow moved forward, he felt a bump under his right tire as though he'd hit something large. He was freaked and wondered if it was something from the spacecraft.

He stopped the plow and tied the string on his parka under his chin. He saw a hand reach upward and pound on the side of the window. Then a second hand appeared, both with four digits on each hand.

Next, he turned on the light inside the cab and a face appeared, eyes staring at him. Then the being ran into the woods and vanished. Without any warning, the creature reappeared in the middle of the road ahead of him. Intuitively, Ross sensed the being was cold and needed shelter. "I offered him to come inside my snowplow, but he wanted nothing to do with it."

Dr. Clarke asked how he communicated with the creature, and Ross said he just understood. The male creature said it was Ross' fault that he was in the cold because the spacecraft took off without him. The creature finally got inside the cab after Ross explained that he had to clear the roads and couldn't leave him in the cold.

Ross told Dr. Clarke how frightened he was. He continued plowing the roads to the 50-mile point and turned around to plow the highway again. Snow continued to fall with four inches on the road. The spacecraft returned in the middle of the road at the exact spot he encountered earlier. The Starman suddenly vanished. Within seconds he stood in front of the craft. Before he vanished, Ross thought he detected a brief and simple salute or wave.

Ross continued his story, "He told me the craft had malfunctioned. They set down in the middle of the road only momentarily for repairs. He was curious and had gone outside to do some testing of the snow. When I came upon them, my appearance shocked them, and in their confusion, they took off without him. They had not expected anyone to appear in the middle of the storm. To add to his dilemma, they were not allowed to make human contact, so he was uneasy about being discovered. So, they immediately took off, leaving him behind. In the process, they violated several rules of their travel. They said they were a young crew and would likely lose their rights as explorers if their superiors discovered their mistake."

Ross added, "That's another thing. He was fascinated with the snowplow and how it worked. He considered it a rather primitive machine but one that he was curious about. He told me that humans put too much reliance on oil-based machines. He said they should spend their energy studying the use of magnetic propulsion for travel. He could not understand why our scientists had not gone in this direction."

Dr. Clarke asked if he could remember anything else about the alien.

"Not much," Ross replied. "The alien was quiet most of the time. I was lost for words. I didn't know what to ask a man from the stars, so I was quiet. After he was gone, I thought of a million questions, but when you are there and it is happening to you, it is different."

He continued to describe the alien. "He was small in

stature. He had a human form, but he wasn't human. He could have passed for maybe a ten-year-old from a distance. His ability to appear and disappear fascinated me. I asked him about it, but he said that everyone in his world could come and go like that. He said I could do it too. I just had to learn to use my brain in the right way. I didn't understand what he meant."

After a moment, Ross thought of something else that puzzled him. "The day after this happened, a couple of military officers showed up at work and asked if anyone had reported strange lights or UFOs on the night of the storm. Of course, his boss told him there were no reports. I had not reported it and neither had Ed, the other driver. I thought it was best to keep quiet, so I never told them about Starman. When the military showed up, I played dumb too. I didn't want to lose my work because of some government investigation. Besides, the military has too much control in this state anyway."

Ross never told the other driver about his encounter. Dr. Clarke never saw Ross again and concluded her research in Alaska in the spring of 2007. Last she heard, Ross no longer drives a snowplow in the winter and was teaching and coaching in a village near his new home.

Orbs over Ninilchik, Alaska

The quiet town of Ninilchik is a great basecamp to explore the many outdoor recreation opportunities available in the Kenai Peninsula, including hiking, fishing, and wildlife viewing. The town boasts amazing views across Cook Inlet, fascinating Russian history, great salmon and halibut fishing, and UFO sightings.

Sheri Liebenthal lives in the fishing village and has indigenous blood. She says they are good people there.

It was a normal evening in 2020 in the village when something unusual was spotted in the sky. Tiffany, Sheri's daughter, ran to their house's front window and saw four bright orange orbs in the sky, bigger than the moon. That's when the two women ran down to the beach to get a closer look as they stood on the dunes. Above them was what they described as a baby light coming down that was joined by eight orbs now hovering in the sky, and all of them merged into one large bright orb and it vanished within seconds.

Sheri was able to record it. The sighting was later debunked as military flares, but Sheri and her daughter and many of the village people knew whatever they had witnessed was out of this world.

Sheri says there are cave drawings in the area that appear to be alien beings.

Alien-looking petroglyphs are located at Whale Pass, Prince of Wales Island

Security Guard records blinking Orb near Fairbanks, Alaska

Jared Augustine is a security guard and one night in May of 2016 while on patrol at 3:00 a.m. he noticed a bright light in the sky and started to record it on his cell phone. The blinking orb dropped from a much larger orb and two orbs shot out from the bottom of it and disappeared. The main light stayed longer and then vanished in the sky. According to Jared, there was no sound. He could only hear birds chirping. He posted his video on YouTube and received positive reviews, but the video seems to have vanished like the UFO orbs he witnessed in 2016.

CHAPTER FOUR

Alaska's Dark Pyramid

A top-secret government facility beneath the Alaskan wilderness may be hiding an extraterrestrial pyramid. Strange forces within the Alaska Triangle are making wildlife more aggressive toward humans. Some believe that a top-secret government facility beneath the Alaskan wilderness may be hiding an extraterrestrial pyramid. There is a black pyramid buried deep underground in the Alaskan wilderness, somewhere between Nome and Mt. McKinley. Exactly twice the size of the Great Pyramid at Giza — itself the tallest known human-made structure for nearly 3,800 years the dark pyramid is guarded by the U.S. military, or by a mysterious private militia that strictly controls access to the site. It is alien technology, or a remnant of a lost human civilization and generates its own energy, which may or may not be electricity. Regardless, it is estimated to be enough to power the entire state of Alaska...or the entire nation of Canada. Indescribably ancient (or a lost invention of Nikola Tesla) it was discovered in the closing months of WWII...or in 1949, or in 1992. And honestly, if you can't find a game hiding somewhere around its perfectly square base, we just don't have much to talk about.

According to Douglas A. Mutschler, geologists had used the detonation to undertake a seismographic study of the earth's crust, only to find "a pyramid structure larger than Cheops" underground, somewhere west of Mount McKinley. Mutschler recalls that the local NBC affiliate ran a story announcing the structure's discovery about 6 months after the detonation, but when Mutschler attempted to follow up with the station to get a copy of the story (evidently not as part of his duties at Fort Richardson) they denied that the story had ever run and asserted that they certainly didn't have a copy to provide. Mutschler then called relatives to track down copies of the story that had run on other stations, but apparently none had: the discovery only appeared on Anchorage's Channel 13.

Douglas Mutschler wrote a letter to Earth Files Investigator Linda Moulton Howe on June 22, 2012. The subject was: "Pyramid under Alaska".

My name is Douglas A. Mutschler, CW2, USA, and I learned that Alaska had an underground pyramid during my tour of service there. After they informed us that this was reported in 1992, I learned of further facts regarding it. I attempted to share this knowledge with others, but I haven't received any feedback. Buried the very day after it was brought to my attention.

The tenacious Mutschler was transferred from Alaska to Fort Meade (the ultra-secret home of the National Security Agency), where he availed himself of classified archives seemingly confirming the pyramid story.

I thought maybe they'd have something about this pyramid. So, I went to what I guess would be like a librarian. And I asked him if he had anything on archaeological sites – I didn't say pyramid. But I said archaeological sites or underground facilities in Alaska.

He said, 'Well, if we do, it might be in container X, Y or Z.' So, I went over there, and I was just looking around and I didn't really find anything saying pyramid, but I grabbed a couple of Alaska–like from two different safes. And I had just sat down and these two guys came, you know, you can feel when someone is standing behind you. And these two goons go, 'Hey, you don't have a need to know for that information.' ...And the other guy somehow in that conversation, he goes, 'They don't want us messing with them up there anymore. They don't want you messing with them up there. They don't want us or anybody messing with them.'

The morning after Linda Moulton Howe's interview with Mutschler, however, things got really weird. Inspired by Mutschler's dogged (but ultimately only partially successful) search, the adopted son of a retired Western Electric engineer reached out to Howe to confirm the basics of Mutschler's claims, and to add several new wrinkles. Howe's new source claimed that his father had worked on a powerful electrical system emanating from a very large underground pyramid *of unknown origin* in Alaska between 1959 and 1961.

Digital Seance details the second (indirect) witness's revelation (name not given)

After the war, he earned a degree in electrical engineering and physics. After finishing college, my father was 're-recruited' by the military to join a group of other experts to study and work at an underground structure in Alaska that in his words they called the 'Dark Pyramid.' He spoke numerous times of how seriously the government took this project and the steps they took to keep it a secret. (I always assumed it was a military installation.) He said it was a study of energy distribution. He went on to be the key leader of the 'information Bubble' for AT&T which of course was the precursor to the web and cell phone technology we all know today.

In his later years, he would always complain when receiving his electric bill that it would be FREE if we knew the truth. Now I'm starting to think he knew a whole lot more than we ever gave him credit for. I am in the process of going through his old papers and studies to see if there is any reference to his time in Alaska. There may be no information since as he said it was 'Confidential.' If this Pyramid allegedly found in 1992 is true, our Gov. may have known about it far earlier than that and had taken extensive measures to keep it hidden.

There aren't any specifics, but its existence was 'accidentally' revealed on a KTVA CBS Channel 11 (Anchorage) newscast back in the 1990s, and that newscast has been utterly scrubbed from the internet and hard copies have been destroyed. Not even the station was permitted to keep a copy of it. Its location is somewhere in a forested area between Denali National Park and Nome, it's mostly underground, it's connected with the military, and it's accessed by an elevator that reaches the surface. That's about all the information known at this time, although it's also possible that the whole thing is a hoax, and the station was deceived into running a story on it.

It's unlikely the story was a hoax, however, since the story disappeared, you can bet it poked a hornets' nest.

CHAPTER FIVE

UFOs and Alien Encounters

On November 17, 1986, one of the best documented UFO cases happened in the skies above Alaska. Three UFOs played tag with Japan Air Lines (JAL) cargo flight 1628 for 50 minutes while they were visually observed by a sometimes-terrified flight crew. During the last 30 minutes the UFOs were tracked on military and civilian radar, and the entire encounter was verified by a high-level administrator of the Federal Aviation Administration (FAA). The incident received media coverage all over the world.

Japan Airlines Captain Kenju Terauchi was an ex-fighter pilot and senior airline pilot with more than 10,000 hours of flight experience. He was assigned to fly a Japan Airlines cargo flight from Paris to Reykjavik, Anchorage, and on to Tokyo.

On November 17, 5:09 pm Alaska time, the Anchorage Air Route Traffic Control Center contacted JAL 1628, which at that time was about 104 miles northeast of Fort Yukon. The flight controller asked the pilot to adjust his heading so the plane would pass south of Fort Yukon and Fairbanks. The copilot turned the plane to the left about 15 degrees. Captain Terauchi, sitting on the left side of the cockpit, saw unidentified lights out his side window to the left and below. He thought they were military planes and ignored them. After a few minutes, he realized that these unidentified aircraft were pacing him.

Flight 1628 contacted the Anchorage Center twice in rapid succession and asked if there were any other aircraft in the area. The Anchorage Center responded that there were no military aircraft and ground radar did not show any aircraft other than Flight 1628. Then the two lights began to move erratically. Terauchi recollected in his official report to the FAA, listed here below and edited for length and clarity:

"The distance from the lights was far enough from us and we felt no immediate danger. I thought perhaps it is a UFO. The lights were still moving strangely. Most unexpectedly two spaceships appeared [directly in front of the plane], shooting off lights. The inside cockpit shined brightly, and I felt [the warmth of the UFO's thrusters'] on my face. Then, three to seven seconds later, the fire from jet engines stopped and became a small circle of lights as they began to fly in level flight at the same speed as we were. The middle of the body of the ship sparked an occasional stream of lights, like a charcoal fire. Its shape was square, flying 500 feet to 1,000 feet in front of us, very slightly higher in altitude than us. Its size was about the same as the body of a DC-8 [similar in size to a Boeing 707].

"It is impossible for any manmade machine to make a sudden appearance in front of a jumbo jet that is flying 910 kilometers per hour and to move along in a formation paralleling our aircraft. But we did not feel threatened or in danger. Honestly, we were simply astounded. I have no idea why they came so close to us.

"There was a pale white flat light in the direction where the ships flew away, [pacing us]. The Anchorage Center replied that they saw nothing on their radar. I set our digital weather radar distance to 20 miles, and radar angle to the horizon. There it was, on the screen: a large, green, round object had appeared seven or eight miles away, in the direction of the object.

"We arrived at the sky above the Eielson Air Force Base and Fairbanks. It was a clear night. We were just above the bright city lights, and we checked the pale white light behind us. There was a silhouette of a gigantic spaceship! We must get away quickly!

A terrified Captain Terauchi, in coordination with the Anchorage Center, attempted evasive maneuvers such as flying in a circle and changing altitude. The gigantic UFO, later described by Terauchi as the size of two aircraft carriers, shadowed Flight 1628 through all maneuvers. Terauchi "wondered and feared as to their purpose." Anchorage Center offered to scramble a military jet, but Captain Terauchi declined the offer fearing unintended consequences of a military confrontation with the UFO. About that time a United Airlines passenger jet flew into the same air zone and was requested by the ATC to get a visual on the situation. Terauchi reported, "When the United plane came by our side, the spaceship disappeared suddenly. The strange encounter ended 150 miles away from Anchorage."

In 1986, John Callahan was FAA Division Chief of the Accidents and Investigations Branch in Washington, DC. About a week after the JAL 1628 incident, he got an urgent call from Alaska. Callahan's recollections were recorded in an interview conducted circa 2000. His comments below are edited here for brevity and clarity.

"I forgot who it was that called, but he says 'We got a problem here. I don't know what to tell the media. The whole [FAA] office is full of the media from Alaska.' '[Callahan asks] What's the problem?' He says, 'It's that UFO!' I said, 'What UFO?' He says, 'Well, last week, we had a UFO chase a 747 across the skies up here for about 30 minutes or so.'

"I told him to get all that data together. I wanted all the [civilian and military] disks that they had and all the tapes that they had available—and flown overnight to the tech center where I'm sitting."

The military refused to send their tapes, but he got everything Anchorage Traffic Control had. We told him that we wanted this room set up to be just like it was an Anchorage. And we wanted all that data to come to this scope [radar monitor], and we want to see everything the controller has seen. We want to hear everything he heard. And we wanted it all tied together – the radar, the digital radar, and the sound. When Callahan played the tapes, he heard a three-way conversation between Anchorage Air

Traffic Control (ATC), Elmendorf's NORAD Regional Operations Control Center (ROCC), and Captain Terauchi of JAL 1628. He also played a tape of the ATC radar sightings on a scope. Anchorage Air Traffic Control didn't see the UFOs on their radar, but based on their conversation, the military was clearly tracking the UFOs. Callahan explained:

"The military controller has what they call height-finding radar, and they have long-range radar and short-range radar, so if they don't catch it on one of their systems, they catch it on the other. Ours wouldn't record it.

"Details reported by the military controller indicated that the UFOs were traveling thousands of miles per hour as they maneuvered in the airspace around the 747. The military controller had one other surprise finding. Near the end of the incident, a United Airlines flight was diverted to observe the JAL flight. By then, Captain Terauchi no longer saw the huge UFO, and the United Pilots did not see it either. Unbeknownst to both of them, the military radar indicated that the UFO had tucked in out of sight behind the United Flight and had begun following it."

After sitting through the presentation, Callahan's boss turned to him and said, "Don't talk to anybody until I give you the okay." The next day his boss set up a briefing. According to Callahan, I brought all the people from the tech center. We went upstairs. We had all kinds of boxes of data that we handed them – printouts. It filled up the room. They brought in three people from the FBI, three people from the CIA, and three people from Reagan's scientific study team, and I don't know who the rest of the people were, but they were all excited. When they asked me what I thought, I told them that it looked like we had a UFO that was up there. They were very, very excited about the data. They had said that this was the only time—and they had used the words 'a UFO'—was ever recorded on radar for any length of time.

Within months of the incident, Captain Terauchi was banished to a desk job because he had "embarrassed" the company. He was fully reinstated a few years later. John Callahan retired from the FAA, became an industry consultant, and periodically recounted the true story of JAL flight 1628.

CHAPTER SIX

Star Traveler Dog

In Dr. Ardy Sixkiller Clarke's book, *Space Age Indians*, she traveled to see an Alaskan man named Arlis who lived in a cabin on the outskirts of an Alaskan village. He was a twenty-eight-year-old veteran of Afghanistan and his life there centered on the thirty sled dogs he kept in his backyard. She met him at a local dog race held each year as a preliminary trial for the sled dog teams that entered regional and statewide competitions. Arlis had named each dog after the star and constellations.

Arlis said it happened the year before after he built his cabin in the Alaska wilderness. By January, the river freezes, and the ice is two to three feet deep. One night he stayed up later than usual to read. As soon as he turned out the light, the whole cabin lit up like daylight outside. A UFO with a circle of white lights outlining it was suspended about twenty feet over the river. Moments later it descended and rested on the river.

Arlis was amazed and afraid to do anything while standing outside. Clarke asked what his dogs were doing. "Nothing, he replied. "Cassiopeia stood on her kennel as if in a trance. I ran back into the house, stood in front of the stove, put on my snowsuit, and headed outside again."

At first, he thought they were people outside the ship checking on something, but they weren't walking on ice. They were skimming it. Their feet didn't touch the ice. They didn't see Arlis at first until his dog Cassiopeia started barking. He pointed his rifle at the one coming toward him who kept telling him that they were friendly and not to fear them. Arlis suddenly dropped his rifle for some unknown reason as one of the beings flew up the bank.

Arlis told Clarke he didn't particularly feel they were friendly although the Star Man kept repeating it. "I was still skeptical. I mean, I live forty miles from town. I don't have a telephone and cells don't work out here. If something happened, I'm on my own." He wondered if they were military because of the bases in Alaska and the possibility they were testing an experimental craft.

Next, Arlis asked them to prove they were friendly. The Star Man picked him up and flew him inside the craft. He took him to an area on the top deck that must have been a control center. "There were all kinds of screens that looked like computers. There were two other beings inside the control center. There were screens built into a panel. Something like Star Trek but not exactly. Two beings were sitting in front of the screens. One seemed to be monitoring what was going on outside. The other one seemed to be a map of the sky. Another showed a view of the area around the cabin. In the center of the room was a clear tower. I saw no levers or means of flying the craft."

The glass wasn't glass but felt more like a strange plastic that melded to his hand and then went back to its original form. He tried again and this time the plastic left his handprint embedded in the material but then reformed to its original shape. It was as big around as a number three washtub and came up out of the floor and touched the ceiling. He said it was the power system of their ship.

Arlis asked the beings how their ships were powered, and they said they received power from the atmosphere to recharge their systems, so they never had to use fuel as we know it.

Arlis said the beings sitting at the screens appeared to be machines or robots. They didn't acknowledge him or talk. He believed his guide was the only living being on the ship, but the rest were robots. He thought the guide was a biological entity because he had two arms, a head, a middle, and two legs but had super strength. On the lower level were his living space and a type of hammock inside that was suspended in the air but was more like a web of silky strands.

Arlis continued, "There were machines in the room, which he indicated were used for nutrition and sleep. There was no desk or books or anything personal. I saw plants in glass containers. I invited him to visit my home, but he declined and said he had a schedule to keep. He said he didn't visit areas with people if it could be avoided. They believed my cabin was abandoned or they would not have chosen this site. He said he would see me again. Then the next thing I know, I'm standing on the bank, watching the ship lift off the ice and go straight upward until it suddenly disappeared."

The others on the ship were not robots but crossbreeds of biological parts and mechanical parts called Synthetics. They were more companions in space because they work in an atmosphere and feel no danger. They do not need to sleep or eat, and they maintain and pilot the spaceship.

"They looked more human. Their skin looked like stretched rubber. There were no lines on their faces like they were wearing a mask. The Star Man looked more human. He was dark-skinned like me. He had round eyes that were larger than human eyes. I never saw his hair. He had a covering over his head that was part of his suit. He was probably six foot three or four. I'm six foot two and he was slightly taller than me. There were instruments attached to his arm around his wrists. I asked him if the instruments were weapons, and he said that he never carried weapons. He did not need weapons."

Clarke asked if the Star Man returned. "Three times. They always come in the winter. They land on the ice and four beings come out. Three were the robot kind and one was my friend. On his second visit, he came into my cabin. He was fascinated by my book collection. He picked up an axe and asked me how I used it. He was interested in a plane that I used to shave logs. He put his finger in my sugar bowl and tasted the sugar. He tasted the salt, too."

They always communicated by telepathy and never spoke the words aloud. On his second visit when he came into the cabin, he saw a small pup that Arlis was caring for. The pup couldn't walk. I brought him inside and hoped that with the warmth from the stove and a massage, I could help him, but the pup was not responsive. He feared he would have to put him down. "When the Star Man saw him, I told him the problem. He picked the pup up and asked me if he could take him. A year later, he returned the pup. He was now strong and healthy. He is one of the best dogs I have for his age. He's a super dog. I call him Star Traveler. He's probably the only sled dog on Earth that has traveled to other worlds."

The Star Man told Arlis that his planet was covered with snow and ice year-round and that the people live in underground cities. They had created an artificial sun underground. At one time, there was a sun, but it burned out and their world went cold, and that's when they moved underground.

While the Star Man was in his house, he noticed the crucifix on the wall and wanted to know what it meant. Arlis explained about God and Jesus, but he did not know God or Jesus in his world. When Arlis showed him the Bible, he didn't understand how it could be the word of God. Arlis expected his space friend to return in January.

Arlis put his experience into perspective for Dr. Clarke. "In our way, we always pray for all the four-leggeds, the two-leggeds, and the winged creatures. So, it is not that I believed in aliens or Star People, it is just that our prayers appear to include every living creature in the universe. It doesn't bother me religiously. I don't believe that God only created man. I don't think my friend means any harm to the Earth. I believe he's nothing more than an explorer like our astronauts. The only thing that bothers me is his secrecy. I ask myself repeatedly why he's unwilling to reveal himself to the world. If he can travel throughout the universe, why not share his knowledge? But then when I think of how his knowledge might be used, I understand."

Clarke asked, "I'm really interested in why you call him a friend. Can you explain?"

"I call him a friend because any man or being who cares enough to save a dog is my friend."

CHAPTER SEVEN

Alaskan Legends

Not only is Alaska's history steeped in fur trading, whale harvesting, and gold mining. It also has ancient petroglyphs on rocks. Because their true meanings are elusive, they remain a mysterious link to people who inhabited the world a long time ago.

Petroglyphs are in abundance in Southeastern Alaska and are unique because they are associated with salmon streams, rather than primitive village sites, and they always face the sea. Mouths of salmon streams are filled with inscriptions pecked into hard rock-like sandstone, slate, and granite, while good rocks for carving remain bare in villages near those streams.

To those familiar with the ancient beliefs and oral traditions of the Tlingit and Haida Indians, the petroglyphs show that salmon is life. These Native Alaskans, whose diet was primarily fish, were not hunters and had no agriculture. If the salmon failed to return, it could mean starvation for the clans. Legend has it that a Tlingit boy named Shin-quo-klah, or "Mouldy End," was punished by the Salmon People for wasting dried salmon. They took him under the sea, but later returned him to his people.

Shin-quo-klah became a great shaman. Legend says that his image is etched on a rock at Karta Bay, placed near where he died after he accidentally killed his own soul which was inhabited by a supernatural salmon at the time. Copies of the etching were all around the beaches of Hydaburg and Wrangell, where it's believed his influence was being used with the Salmon People to insure adequate runs of salmon.

Petroglyphs also appear in the Kodiak Archipelago, where at least seven sites have carvings that depict human figures, animal forms, and geometric designs. There are four large clusters of petroglyphs at Cape Alitak, at the entrance to Alitak Bay. Some Alaskans think that the designs were made to mark territory, to act as permanent signs that linked families with subsistence harvesting areas.

The oldest rock drawings appear to have been carved as early as 10,000 years ago, and archaeologists have found similar abstract symbols along the coast of Siberia. There is no way to discern the true intent or motivation of the artists, but the drawings are one of the few sources of ancient art that tie Alaska Natives to their heritage.

There's a strange beach in Alaska called Petroglyph Beach, near the small town of Wrangell. The small chunk of coastline is home to roughly 40 petroglyphs, now a state historic park since the year 2000. The petroglyphs can mean many things, from land markers and hunting sights to religious symbols and markings, but unfortunately there is no true way of knowing for sure what these historic etchings may mean.

A huge-eyed being looks at the world at Petroglyph Beach

Perhaps the legend of Shin-quo-klah is more than a legend, and the shaman was abducted by aliens and taken to their underground base. Hundreds have witnessed UFOs and UAPs (unidentified aerial phenomena) diving into the ocean, and some people claim they have been taken to undersea UFO bases.

In Raymond Fowler's book, *The Watchers II*, Betty Andreasson Luca described how she was taken by the little grays to a deep undersea place. Under hypnosis, Betty described a city of crystal reminiscent of the *Wizard of Oz* movie where Dorothy enters an Emerald City. Betty told author, Raymond Fowler, how UFO occupants took her to the "Green Realm," a sunless land or island of fog and mist. This place was inhabited by lemur-like creatures and the place contained a pyramid with crystal walkways and bridges over water. When Fowler asked Betty if she had left the Earth, Betty replied: "I believe we were in space, and somehow we were in the center of the Earth."

Everything she touched came to life—like living water. Was Betty shown a holographic world or a real undersea crystal city in the deepest regions of our oceans where everything shapeshifts?

CHAPTER EIGHT

Undersea ET Bases

There are many undersea areas around the world believed to have bases where extraterrestrials conduct their experiments. Southern California continues to have reports of UAP (Unidentified Aerial Phenomenon) tracked by the Navy. UAPs or USOs have been witnessed diving into the ocean at incredible speeds.

An underwater alien base may be located off the coast of the quiet Alaskan town of Ketchikan, an Alaskan port city facing the *Inside Passage*, a popular cruise route along the state's southeastern coast. It's known for its many Native American totem poles, on display throughout town. Nearby Misty Fiords National Monument is a glacier-carved wilderness featuring snowcapped mountains, waterfalls, and salmon spawning streams. It's also home to black bears, wolves, bald eagles, and UFOs—lots of them.

Terry Pyles, an artist, witnessed a fireball in the sky with his wife while on the deck of their home one night. It looked like spinning molten metal with lights rotating around it. The UFO was totally silent.

Ufologists believe that the U.S. Navy's presence there and their top-secret nuclear submarines indicate that they are tracking UAPs in the area and deep in the ocean where an alien base might exist.

The waterway is the home of the United States Navy's Southeast Alaska Acoustic Measurement Facility, more commonly known as SEAFAC. Built-in 1991, it's located roughly 675 miles from the major submarine bases in Washington State. For years it seems its existence was kept relatively hush-hush, although locals clearly knew a major submarine testing facility had been established. But to this very day, the place catches people off-guard. I have received roughly a half-dozen emails over the years from various individuals, from pilots to visitors to the area, who wondered why they saw a huge submarine plowing the waters in a fjord near Ketchikan. SEAFAC is a highly classified top-secret operation where new technologies and equipment configurations are tested aboard multi-billion-dollar American nuclear submarines and where their acoustic signature is measured while underway.

Behm Canal is an ideal setting for an underwater acoustic test range because it is shielded from the ocean and large amounts of vessel traffic, and thus from ambient noise. Its basin is also ideal, with a smooth tub-like contour that provides as close to lab-like acoustic conditions as possible. It can also be cordoned off relatively easily when tests are underway.

The facility allows for static and dynamic acoustic tests, the latter of which can take place throughout the submarine's performance envelope. Two acoustic arrays are attached to the seafloor, which has a depth of roughly 1250 feet, to capture a submarine's audible signature as it travels back and forth across the canal while executing various test profiles.

A data analysis site and general base of operations is located on Back Island which sits on the eastern edge of the restricted test area.

Could the Navy's top-secret operations be involved with extraterrestrials, and know they have an undersea base off the coast? If the nearest U.S. Naval base is located in Washington State, nearly 750 miles distance from the Ketchikan area, what are Naval submarines doing in Ketchikan?

Jonny Enoch is an author, journalist, researcher of prehistoric civilizations, and a futurist who explores mysteries around the world. He has seen UFOs and believes the military and aliens are colluding on projects in the waters of K. He wonders if alien reverse technology is being used by the U.S. Navy in exchange for something the aliens want—biology or even human abductees.

What if the extraterrestrials on Earth are at least one thousand years or more ahead of our technology and can travel through wormholes and access the past and the future? The possibilities are endless with such technology, including altering timelines for their benefit.

Perhaps they even possess such advanced technology to pass from one dimension to another.

The Gulf of Alaska, like the Bermuda Triangle, and other deep ocean areas like Southern California offer excellent hiding places and bases for extraterrestrial species.

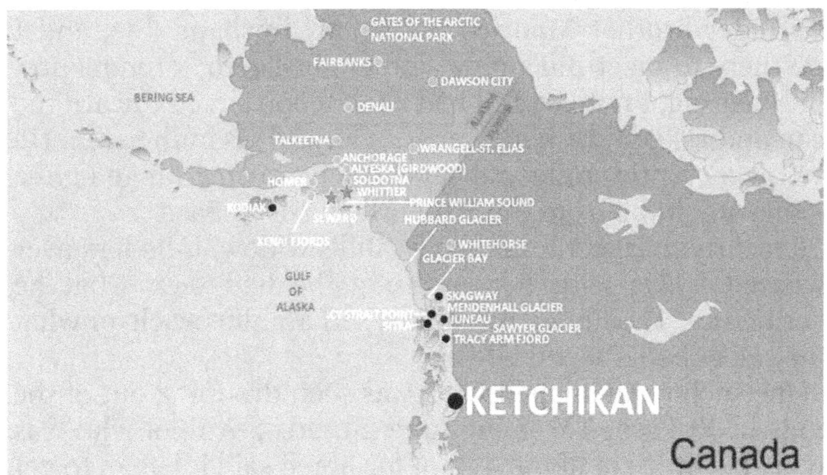

Eric Hecher explores the Waters off Ketchikan

UFO researcher Eric Hecher decided to find out if there are any anomalies in the bay area near Ketchikan. He took a boat and put a hydrophone in the water. Eric detected only the organic sounds of waves and bubbles. But he takes the recording to Kurt Reiman, an audio expert in Anchorage, and listens to a spectrogram.

At first, Kurt hears only the idling of the boat, water, and bubbles rising from the ocean floor. Then he nears something unusual and sees a single line on the graph that is electronically created. It isolated the anomaly as the sound continues 7 minutes, rising in pitch and then down again. Kurt feels that an object moved under Eric's boat and then departed. A USO (unidentified submerged object)?

Southern California's Alien Undersea Base

Alaska isn't the only place on the planet that has UFO reports off the coast of Southern California and witnessed by U.S. military ships and people who live in California. The first time I had heard about UFO activity off the coast of Southern California was from my newly acquired step-uncle, William Peter Blatty, author and screenwriter of the best-selling novel, *The Exorcist*. The year was 1974. My mother, her husband, Bill's older brother Maurice Blatty, my husband Joe, and I were there to meet Bill's new wife Linda Tuero, a tennis pro. While visiting, I noticed Bill had a telescope aimed toward the ocean and asked if he had ever seen any UFOs in the area. He gave me a cryptic smile and said, "I have seen strange lights, but they might be from the Point Magu Naval Base.

Recently, I asked Julie Blatty, Bill's widow, if he had ever discussed UFOs with her. In 1983, he had seen what he described as "The Flying Breadbox," off Malibu beach, or what some call cubed-shaped UFOs.

One such cube-shaped UFO was seen dropping out of the clouds in El Paso, Texas on June 29, 2015. A man who was leaving his office at about 1 p.m. for lunch said it began to get very windy that day. He noticed that the center of some swirling clouds became "jet black."

Just as the man snapped the photo, a massive, cube-shaped UFO appeared, "jetting out of this worm-hole type manifestation." A woman who works as an accountant at an El Paso office also reported seeing the cube, which she described as "sinister," in a telephone interview with Secureteam10. "It stopped me in my tracks completely," the woman said. "I remember a magnetic humming sound that emanated from this thing. It was really scary." In a telephone interview with the woman who claimed she saw the black-cube UFO, Secureteam10 asked her what she would say to skeptics who call the sighting a hoax.

"All I can say is I was there and saw this thing with my own two eyes," the woman said. "I personally took a picture of it.... I hope that by doing this interview can confirm this did happen. No one is going to tell me different, for sure."

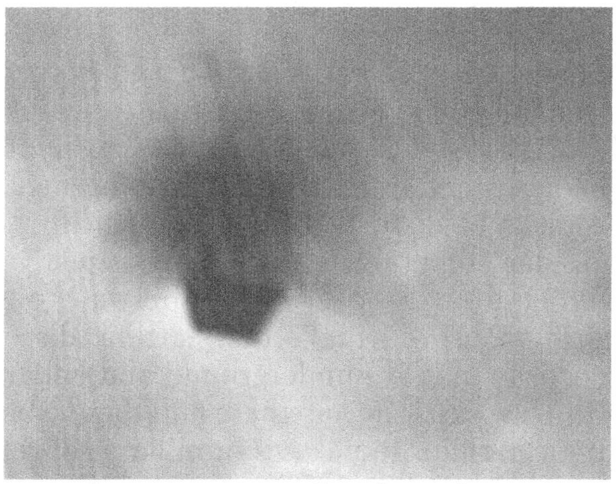

El Paso, Texas cube-shaped UFO

Expedition X Investigates Catalina UFO Mystery

Jessica Chobot and Phil Torres are investigators on the Josh Gates *Expedition X* series for the Discovery Channel. In 2021, they visited Catalina Island, 22 miles off the coast of Los

Angeles, to investigate all the UFO sightings and continued sightings by Naval ships doing maneuvers in the area in Season 3, Episode 6.

Jessica and Phil hired a boat to take them out to an area of the ocean near Catalina Island that has shown high magnetic readings. This time they used an ROV meter to scan the ocean floor at 1,000 feet to see if anything was there. "ROV" stands for "remotely operated vehicle;" ROVs are unoccupied, highly maneuverable underwater machines that can be used to explore ocean depths while being operated by someone at the water's surface. They weren't getting readings until something showed up on the ROV monitor. There was a sudden flash and the ROV froze.

Meanwhile, Jessica was onshore observing the boat and Phil when suddenly a white object rose from the sea near the boat and went straight up in the sky and vanished.

Jessica and Phil realized that they had stirred upset the undersea occupants and they didn't like it. There were no magnetic anomalies after the UFO ascended into the sky at an incredible rate of speed from the spot the ROV had found it at 1,000-foot depth. The ROV was not harmed by the flash, but whatever technology the beings used, made the water vehicle inoperable for a moment while the craft escaped into the sky.

These beings, whether alien or terrestrial beings, watch us but don't want to be disturbed from their earthly bases. And least of all, they don't like Naval Ships and Navy Pilots conducting their exercises over their underwater bases.

In time, humans will make the startling discovery that these beings have massive underground and undersea bases throughout the world. They are here and they've been here a very long time, perhaps thousands or millions of years before we appeared on Earth. Buckle up—disclosure is near.

MUFON Ann Druffel's UFO Journal on Catalina UFOs

I included Ann Druffel's journals about her UFO sightings off the Southern California Coast from my prior book, *Extraterrestrial Encounters of the Extraordinary Kind,* because of her first hand sightings over the years. Ann's sightings confirm aliens do have undersea bases in Earth's deepest oceans. Since the recent UFO sightings by Navy pilots off the coast of Southern California and Catalina Island, I felt it was important to honor my friend, author, and MUFON investigation Ann Druffel with her journals on UFO sightings through the years that she and her mother witnessed over Southern California as well as other witnesses and the accounts of strange sightings in the sky. Again, I include her notes on her encounters.

My first meeting with Ann was in 1981 at my Los Angeles apartment when she heard about my parent's UFO encounter in 1950 and contacted me to conduct a regressive hypnosis session with my mom and me. It was in the summer of 1984 that Ann and I reconnected when we both were volunteering at Stephan A. Schwartz's Mobius Society in Los Angeles, dedicated to remote viewing in archaeology and other psychic experiments with well-known psychics. Ann and I continued to stay in touch through the years and she always honored me as a guest on my talk show *Rainbow Visions*. We remained friends until her death on June 12, 2020, at age ninety-three. Ann was my inspiration to continue research into UFO and alien abduction phenomena and other Earth mysteries.

Ann authored six books and contributed 190 plus pieces to the field's top UFO journals. Her "grand opus" book was *Firestorm: Dr. James E. McDonald's Fight for UFO Science,* published in 2003, re-introducing the phenomenal UFO research and results of the atmospheric physicist, James E. McDonald during his work in the UFO field between 1966 and 1971. McDonald made great strides in convincing the scientific community that UFOs were a real phenomenon that had been neglected by science. He was on the verge of breaking through the government coverup when he died suddenly. Ann felt that his untimely death in 1971 may not have been suicide, but murder due to the information he had uncovered about UFOs.

Ann's two other books included her extensive investigation into the alien abduction of women who lived in the Tujunga Canyon of Southern California in her book, *The Tujunga*

Canyon Contacts, and her book *How to Defend Yourself Against Alien Abduction.*

Ann's first UFO sighting happened in 1945 when she was a young girl. She viewed a bright yellowish object in a clear blue sky over Long Beach, California. She and her mother, Mrs. Elroy, observed the object as it slowly traveled west. After an hour and a half, having traveled about thirty degrees NNE to NNW, it released fifteen to twenty small shiny objects, each taking varying paths out and away from the main object. This sighting coincided when the first experimental atomic bomb exploded in New Mexico. This event most likely set Ann on her quest to uncover the mystery of UFOs and alien abductions.

Keep in mind that Navy pilots observed a "Tic Tac" UFO one hundred miles off the coast of Southern California in 2004 while they were conducting maneuvers (refer to Chapter 4). Southern California has been a hotbed of UFO activity for over 70 years.

Santa Catalina Channel "Cloud Cigars" by Ann Druffel

Since 1962 there have been recurring sightings of so-called cloud-cigars over the Catalina Channel in Southern California. The hovering, seemingly energized clouds are reported both day and night and are accompanied by sightings of smaller, disc-like objects miles inland, while the larger objects remain high above the Pacific Ocean between the mainland and Catalina Island, twenty (20) miles off the coast. Available facts indicate the possibility that the small craft "materialized" within the developing cloud.

The transitory nature of UFOs dismayed researchers. The objects appeared to startle witnesses and in most cases were gone before any permanent record of their passage could be obtained. (Keep in mind that during the 1960s, cell phones were not available. The first cell phone was invented in 1973.)

In rare instances, however, the appearance of UFOs can be predicted because of the reoccurrence of sightings in certain regions. One of the regions is over the Pacific Ocean between the coast of Southern California and the offshore islands, notably Santa Catalina Island, which lies about twenty miles west of the mainland.

We are concerned specifically here with a rectangular area between thirty-three (33) degrees and thirty-four (34) degrees latitude north between one-hundred-nineteen (119) degrees and one-hundred seventeen point five (11.7.5) degrees longitude west. Other "channel" and "basin" areas named for the cities and islands associated with them are involved here in question, which is more meaningful. In most cases, the objects were viewed between the mainland and the large offshore island of Santa Catalina by Ann and those she interviewed through the years.

The complex seafloor off Southern California is becoming one of the best-known submarine areas of the world. Data on the topography, sediments, rock formations, and seismic character have been published in several sources. There has typically always been poor navigational control in this area, but it is difficult to correlate this fact with the numerous magnetic anomalies existing here.

The following material has never been published or has never been collected together before in cogent form. It is incomplete and speculative, according to Ann. When viewed as a whole, however, it might allow the UFO research field to study long-lived UFO phenomena with scientific instrumentation.

Ann's 1962 Mystery

The first hint that the sky in the Santa Catalina Channel held more than seagulls occurred, to the best of our knowledge, in August 1962. Two women witnesses, of which this author [Druffel] was one, had brought their six small children, ages eight to one year, for a leisurely day at the Long Beach, California seashore. At about 2:00 p.m. one of the women (including Druffel) noticed a small, white rectangular cloud, which looked exactly like a newly formed section of vapor trail. It seems to be neatly sliced off at each end and transplanted in the blue, smogless sky. Its apparent diameter was about four millimeters at arm's length, and its width was one-half its length.

It was positioned at about forty (40) degrees elevation, approximately one hundred ninety-five (195) degrees azimuth (magnetic) high in the sky. It seemed about midway between the shore and the island of Santa Catalina, which was visible to the south and southwest.

There was no evidence of high-flying jets and no other vapor trails or clouds in the quadrant of the sky. After about fifteen minutes, the witness [Druffel] became aware that it was not a normal vapor trail. It was too short, too isolated, and did not change shape or size in the slightest. Neither did it move in any direction despite a brisk wind blowing on the seashore].

The witness called her friend, Mrs. James (Aileen) Cummings's attention to it, and the two women continued to observe the small white rectangle. For about thirty more minutes it remained motionless, unchanged in size and shape. Then something began to occur within the tiny cloud. Its white vapor began to "churn," presenting an impression of internal activity. It enlarged two or three times—the time was now about 3:15 p.m. During the next half hour, it slowly changed into an oval, twenty to thirty (20-30) times its original size. It still hovered at forty (40) degrees elevation at the original azimuth, but now its apparent diameter had blossomed to four (4) centimeters in length and about two (2) centimeters in width at arm's length. It was solid appearing, unlike a normal cloud. Its vaporous oval shape was definite, and at no time did the edges dissipate beyond the perimeter.

There was a constant churning motion all over the visible surface, somewhat like water boiling in slow motion. The object seemed angled at approximately twenty-five to thirty degrees; its longest diameter being positioned to the witnesses' right. The mysterious sight kept the witnesses' attention, mainly because it seemed that "something" was inside its vaporous exterior. At times it seemed as though the object were about to "open up" to reveal whatever might be lurking within. About forty-five minutes after the formation of the oval, the witnesses saw flashes of light coming from the object. The flashes were bright white and momentary. They extended about a diameter's length out from the surface.

They gave the impression of strong reflections from the bright sun off a metallic surface in the cloud, or it was electric discharges. There was no sound heard. The flashes were periodic, separated by minutes, with no regular rhythm.

During the time the flashes were observed, numerous military jet trails were seen in the south, evidently over and beyond Catalina Island. None of the jet trails appeared within thirty degrees of the churning, flashing cloud. However, these trails indicated the presence of several highly active military jets. After watching the flashes in the cloud for about fifteen minutes, the witnesses approached a nearby lifeguard, hoping he could lend them binoculars so they could get a closer view of the activity within the cloud. He denied having binoculars, and when the witnesses tried to explain to him about the strange cloud, he showed no interest.

At about 5:00 p.m. the witnesses collected their small children, preparatory to making the long thirty-five-mile drive back to their Pasadena homes. They left reluctantly, pausing several times during the quarter mile walk to their cars to stare at the object. It still hung motionlessly high in the sky. They discussed reporting the incident to the *Long Beach Press-Telegram* but rationalized that the object must have been seen and reported by many others. It had been in view for more than three hours. However, there was never any media coverage of the event, to the witnesses' surprise.

As awed as the witnesses felt over the cloud's strange exterior, the activity within it was so inexplicable that both felt inadequate to even verbalize it. Consequently, it went unreported until this date. They remained unaware of the possible significance of the occurrence until years later.

The 1968 "Cloud-Cigar Incident"

The second instance of a "vaporous cloud" over the Catalina Channel occurred on July 9, 1968. By this time, the Los Angeles NICAP Subcommittee [to which Ann Druffel belonged] had established SKYNET, a tracking-and-filter center designed to collect and investigate public UFO reports.

On that summer evening, the phones rang off their hook at the Project Coordinator's [Druffel's] home in Pasadena. Thirty air miles south in Long Beach and surrounding communities, citizens began reporting a large, glowing mass positioned high over the Catalina Channel. Accompanying the silent, hovering cloud were several glowing, smaller globes that maneuvered in the same area of sky.

The first call came from a group of five teenagers gathered at the home of Kevin Allgreen, three miles north of the shoreline. At 9:35 p.m. they had noticed a gray-white, diamond-shaped haze under the full moon in the south-southeast. At 10:05 p.m. it began moving fifty-five degrees in a horizontal line toward the west. By 10:15 it had returned, intact, to its original position near the moon.

Maneuvering near the large object were five smaller cloud-like objects, oval-shaped with clear-cut edges. Two of these were grayish and three were "kind of white." The boys, ages thirteen to eighteen years, viewed the objects through binoculars, and determined that all the unknown masses looked "solid." They kept their shape and precise edges through subsequent maneuvers. Although the edges of the larger object were "fuzzy," it did not seem to be a normal cloud because it moved too fast during its brief journey westward and back again, traveling fifty-five degrees in three minutes. It was many times the size of the smaller balls, an estimated five to six (5-6) times the diameter of the full moon. The end facing west was long and narrow, and the part facing east was shaped "like a diamond."

The boys were convinced that they were viewing something highly unusual. They estimated the main mass was about ten miles high. At approximately 11:00 p.m. the large object turned reddish-orange and began traveling upward at an approximate angle of thirty degrees. By 11:30 p.m. it "just faded away," taking five minutes to dissipate out of sight.

Following up on the teenagers' first call, the family of Mr. Castano of Compton who is also called SKYNET. From their home, seven miles north of Long Beach, the witness and his family had viewed a group of four oval, cloud-like objects the size of pinheads at arm's length, or about one-eighth the size of the full moon. First seen at 9:30 p.m. and disappearing at 10:00 p.m. they were glowing white with precise edges. They were gathered around the moon when first seen, and then started departing "right and left." They seemed to be far out in space. The objects spread out and then dashed toward one another," Castano related. "'It looked like some kind of war." To Mr. Castano, who had never believed in the existence of UFOs before, the event was completely mystifying.

The Castanos did not describe the large cloud, but this is probably because he was much further north than the Long Beach witnesses. Was he seeing the smaller related objects on a mission inward from the Channel?

Another report which seems to validate the above speculation comes from the files of Paul Wilson, another local UFO researcher. He was informed by his neighbors, Michael and Leslie, that they had seen a glowing UFO between 9:30 and 10:00 p.m. on the same night. It traveled toward their home in Hawthorne (fifteen air miles northwest of Long Beach), approaching from the east. It was oval and slightly smaller than the full moon. It was shiny white with clear-cut edges, seemed to be several miles away, and traveled toward the south away from the moon and back again. It was soundless, spun in an apparent circle "around the moon" and afterward let off streams of smoke or vapor from its side. The duration of the sighting was twenty minutes.

From the similarities in the description of the Castano and G. families, it might be assumed that they were viewing the smaller objects during a foray inland. The Castanos saw four objects and the G's witnessed one. We might speculate that the five small objects associated with the main cloud mass had split up into two groups, while the parent object or "cloud cigar" hovered high over the Pacific.

While all this activity was going on, SKYNET was making frantic efforts to obtain additional witnesses and documentation. The only SKYNET member residing near the coast was Jim Griebel who was contacted. His home was three miles north of the Long Beach witnesses. Through binoculars, he could see a cloud-like conglomeration low on the southerly horizon. Whether composed of one or two masses he was not sure, but the mass(es) seemed diamond-shaped on one end and rounded on the other. The bright light from the moon dissipated Griebel's view, but there seems little doubt that he was seeing the primary cloud object which was being viewed from Long Beach. Including Griebel, there were twelve witnesses in all, from four independent groups, who reported on the July 9th, 1968 event.

Nothing about the above cases seemed to click into place at the time of their occurrence. The 1962 case remained an enigma for thirteen years, shoved back into the inner recesses of the two witnesses' minds. That "something" could appear from almost "nothing" and retain shapes, position, and activity for over three hours was inexplicable. The 1968 case, which lasted at least an hour and one-half, was considered a possible "cloud-cigar." This UFO-type is described by Aime Michel in his classic book, *Flying Saucers, and the Straight-Line Mystery*.

The Enigma of 1973

On December 20, 1973, another mystery occurred over the Pacific Ocean between the mainland and Catalina Island. This sighting was as bizarre and long-lived as the two which had gone before. Although at first glance it appeared unassociated with the vaporous masses in the first two events, further study has convinced this author [Ann Druffel] that all three phenomena have many factors in common. Therefore, the three cases are being presented together so that opinions can be sought from other researchers.

At 2:15 a.m. on December 20, 1973, Michael Wagner of Pacific Palisades noticed a yellow glowing "blob" hovering in the south-southeast at an elevation of approximately twenty (20) degrees. He called it to the attention of Robert B. Klinn, known in the UFO community as a skilled researcher. Their viewing position was about twenty miles northwest of Long Beach.

The two witnesses took turns studying the light through a 16-power Navy spyglass, which they were able to steady on a ledge at Klinn's residence. As seen through the telescope, the "blob" resolved into a precise arrangement of round, yellow-gold lights. Though the entire mass appeared larger than Venus with the naked eye, through the 'scope the lights encompassed an area of approximately three millimeters. They were arranged in a vertical column bisecting a horizontal column of equal length. Additional columns of light appeared and arranged themselves into a nearly perfect light-studded triangle. The witnesses adjusted the telescope, and when Klinn again looked through it about three minutes later, the complex of lights had assumed the shape of a huge, cigar-shaped "machine."

Its edges were clear-cut against the sky. Along its side was a horizontal row of about five huge, fiery round lights along the length of the object. These lights were very much larger and brighter than the ones observed earlier; in fact, the entire object had expanded in size at least twenty times.

Each light held tremendous activity within it, "as if looking inside a boiling steel furnace, and even more so." Their primary color was yellow, but many other colors were visible in their teeming mass. As the witnesses watched astounded, the first light ballooned up "like a critical explosion" and smashed through the light directly to its right. That one, in turn, seemed to flare up, as did each in the entire row, as the first fireball traversed the entire row. At the extreme right, the fiery, explosive light paused and pulsated about twice per second; then the smashing reaction returned along the row of lights from right to left. The entire trip back and forth took an estimated thirteen seconds.

As this was happening, a fin-shaped appendage with a vertical row of smaller yellow lights was moving back and forth along the top of the cigar-shaped object "in a very mechanical way." Meantime, the entire object, which now covered more than one and one-half centimeters in the scope's field of view, was moving slowly westward at an estimated five degrees per hour. Toward the end of the sighting, which lasted about one and one-half hours, the object changed shape once more. The appendage on top widened, the lights flickered out, and the object became a darkened cone-shape with a rounded bottom. One faint red light blinked with a regular rhythm on the top. Then the object faded from view at 3:37 a.m.

Attempts at Correlation

The July 1968 manifestation seemed to fit into a recognized UFO class, that of the so-called cloud cigar, widely assumed to be a conglomerate of smaller discs, alternate names being "carrier craft" or "mother ship." But the 1962 and 1973 sightings aren't easily categorized. Both objects changed shape, grew larger and more complex, and demonstrated intense internal activity reminiscent of electrical discharges of high intensity. Is it possible that the 1962 sighting, and the 1973 sighting as well, were incidents of "materialization" into our space-time?

In trying to determine with witness Bob Klinn the possibility that what he had seen was related in some way to the 1962 and 1968 objects, Klinn pointed out that there was no cloud or vapor associated with it. He felt that the 1973 object was a metallic structure and that he was viewing the clashing spheres through "holes" of some kind in its side.

To this author's mind, for the 1973 witnesses to view the activity in its entirety, the side of the object might have been transparent or otherwise open to view. Is it possible that the object was not metallic, but some sort of solid, though transparent, material? Could they have been viewing a similar type of cigar-shaped solid structure that had been surrounded by thick haze during the summer sightings of 1962 and 1968?

Underwater Alien Base off the coast of Malibu

California has one of the largest UFO sightings in the United States. Based on images obtained on Google Earth, a little more than 6 miles off the coast of Point Dume, California, there is an unusual-looking structure on the seabed floor. It's an oval-shaped object with a huge flat top and what appeared to be pillars or columns that seem to reveal the entrance to a darker, inner place. The anomaly is approximately 2,000 feet below the surface of the water, measuring nearly three miles wide. Could this explain the higher percentage of UFOs and USOs (Unidentified Submerged Objects) sightings over Southern California and off the coast as well as abduction stories?

Well-known host Jimmy Church of his *Fade to Black* radio show and substitute host on Coast-to-Coast AM is always one to jump on an exclusive story. He told Huffington Post that one of his listeners named Maxwell contacted him with a Google Earth image showing something odd, underwater off the coast of Malibu. A graphic designer named Dale Romero captured the many angled images (photograph below).

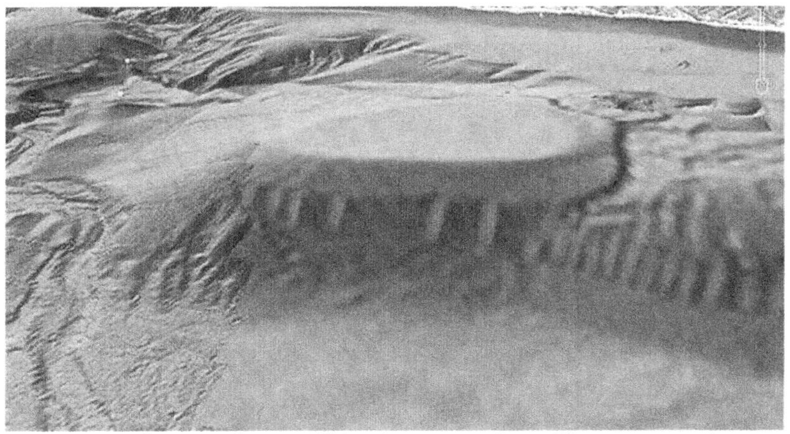

Google Earth Satellite image of Malibu anomaly

It appeared to be like a Greek building with pillars or vertical columns, and it's perfectly oval with a black separation or outline to it and a flat roof. The Google Earth coordinates put it at **34° 1'23.31"N 118° 59'45.64"W.**

Earthquake geologist David Schwartz of the U.S. Geological Survey said after studying the images, "I didn't see anything special about it. I think it's because it looks like there's a flat surface and then, below it, it looks like there are these vertical columns, so somebody can say, 'Oh, this is the entryway to something special,' I think it's natural and is a part of the continental shelf," Schwartz told HuffPost. "It's just a complicated part of what's now offshore that has seen some erosion and, maybe, slumping when perhaps this was partially exposed when the sea level was lower. This is a really major earthquake area and perhaps some of these features are a result of slope failures, due to shaking."

Schwartz added, "There's no flag under the water that says: 'I'm the entrance to an alien base.' Nothing is unnatural-looking about it—it's just showing some sort of variation in the offshore coastal morphology."

Schwartz also shared with HuffPost a research paper published in 2009 by the Geological Society of America, showing cross-sections of the anomaly area. The following image is from that paper. If you look to the left of the middle of the illustration, you can see the oval-shaped "anomaly" some refer to as an underwater UFO base.

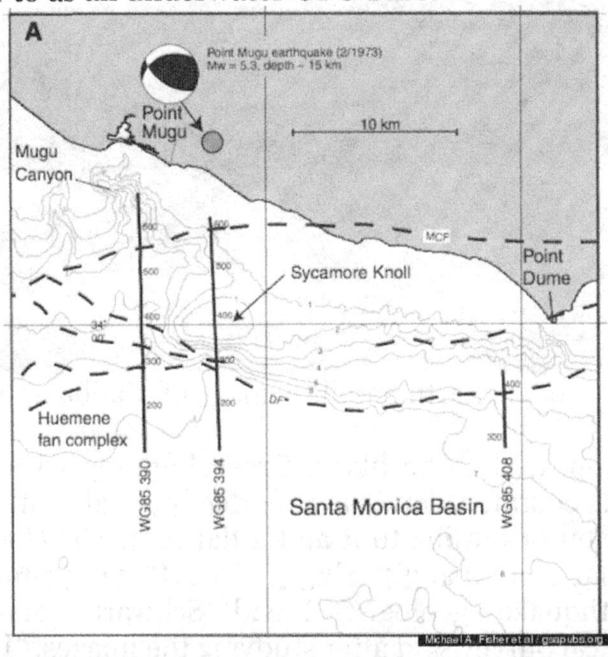

"This is interpreted as a thrust fault," Schwartz explained, "meaning one side of the crust moves up over the other — and what we're looking at is interpreted as being the surface expression of this Dume thrust, which is part of a large fault system in Southern California."

The bottom line, he added, "is that people have recognized this."

HuffPost reached out to John Anthony West, an independent Egyptologist, who won an Emmy award for his research for the 1993 NBC documentary, *Mystery of the Sphinx,* in which he and geologist Robert Schoch presented evidence that the Great Sphinx of Giza might be thousands of years older than previously thought.

West examined the images of the Malibu underwater object and said, "The pictures are a bit misleading in that it looks as though it's on the shore," West told HuffPost. "My first reaction, knowing that it was 2,000 feet under the water, was that under no circumstances could it be artificial—manmade. And I have enough experience, looking at geology and distinguishing between what could perhaps be artificial, and then there's sort of a gray area in-between. As far as I'm concerned, there's no gray area."

West says he's inclined to go along with the geological explanation. "It doesn't look at all manmade. It has what looked like pillars there, but they're unevenly spaced, and then, to the right, you see other seeming pillars still attached, actually, to the bedrock, in the process of forming."

And yet, West acknowledges Unidentified Flying Objects. "I'm convinced that UFOs are a reality—there's too much evidence out there. Beyond that, we don't know anything. We don't know who they are, why they're here, [or] how much of this stuff is our government. A point beyond that is that anything that isn't explained or that can't be explained by current scientific methods, automatically it's aliens. It's the explanation of last resort, and I just don't buy that."

Also weighing in on the Malibu mystery was former FBI Special Agent Ben Hansen who has an extensive background investigating and analyzing questionable pictures and videos. Hansen supplied HuffPost with the following Google Earth image of the underwater object in question: "This was taken from a different angle of the 'mysterious base,'"

Hansen told HuffPost in an email. "The dark areas that people are saying look like the inside of the base really starts to look just like the shading of indentations to the shelf, and the 'pillars' are now represented as jagged ridges."

Hansen cautions about how we interpret things we see on Google Earth. "Google obtains its underwater data from several different sources, including satellite radar and echo sonar from the Navy, NOAA, NASA, and other agencies. Because they often use very different technologies, the derived information isn't always going to agree. When it doesn't, Google relies on its automatic 3D auto-generation programs to make sense of it.

"We're dealing with limited information to render the graphic because we can see it evidenced in the disparity of image quality between the anomaly and the areas immediately surrounding it," Hansen added. "The blurry sections and jagged edges obviously suggest a patchwork of image processing has taken place."

In the end, we're left with a variety of theories to explain the Malibu anomaly. Will the UFO-alien-underwater-base proponents be eventually proven right, leaving geologists in the deep blue dust, scratching their heads and wondering how *they* got it wrong?

West conceded the possibility that the object could be a natural entrance, in the same way, that the action of moving water can form caves below the surface. "There's no big mystery to this thing 2,000 feet under the sea in terms of it being an entrance," West said. "Of course, until you get a camera there, you don't know where the entrance is leading. I'd hazard a guess that it doesn't go in too far, and if they do get in there, I think the chances are that they're not going to find the lost treasures of Atlantis."

Several friends confided through the years that they had witnessed UFOs moving silently over the area. As I described earlier in this book, my step-uncle, author, director, and producer William "Bill" Blatty, known for his best-selling book *The Exorcist*, lived in Malibu during the 1970s and observed UFOs entering the ocean some distance from his beach home. Ann Druffel had numerous sightings of UFOs off the coast of Southern California and her investigations into people abducted by aliens in the Tujunga Canyon area since the mid-1940s is a good indication that aliens are based off the coast of California. Sightings of USOs or UAPs (Unidentified Aerial Phenomena) throughout the world's oceans have existed for hundreds of years. Having an underwater base would certainly make it easier for aliens to come and go without detection.

The day began as a routine naval training exercise. But it would soon become one of the most unusual and baffling UFO sightings of the 21st century involving the United States Navy.

The witnesses included highly trained military personnel—among them several experienced radar operators and fighter pilots who at the time of the sightings were at the controls of the most advanced flight technology ever created.

In 2017, actor Rob Lowe and his two sons chartered the Bold Horizon research vessel to investigate the bizarre Malibu anomaly for their paranormal show *The Lowe Files*. Rob, and his two sons Mathew and John Owen wanted to see if an alien base existed at a depth of 2,000 feet. All of them were skeptical. A ROV (remotely operated vehicle) was employed and then suddenly blacked out at a depth of 1,619 feet and suddenly came back on in the dark ocean water. The submersible sent back images of a natural rock ledge, but no images of the entire anomaly. The scientists and MUFON investigator Chase Kloetzke concluded that nothing alien existed off the coast of Malibu—just a huge natural formation. Rob Lowe heard there is tunnels under Los Angeles and underwater, and still thinks they exist. The show only lasted one season.

Did aliens interfere with the ROV and give them a false image to hide the entrance to their underwater base? Don't count out anything when it comes to alien technology.

U.S.S. Nimitz UFO Encounter off San Diego, California

The date was November 14, 2004, and the location was the Pacific Ocean, about 100 miles southwest of San Diego,

California. The *USS Nimitz* Carrier Strike Group, which included the nuclear-powered carrier and the missile cruiser *USS Princeton*, was conducting a series of drills before deployment in the Persian Gulf.

At about 2 p.m., two F/A-18F Super Hornet fighter jets from the *Nimitz* received an unusual order from an operations officer aboard the *Princeton*. Already airborne, the pilots were told to stop their training maneuvers and proceed to new coordinates for a "real-world" task.

More ominously, the officer asked if they were carrying live weapons. They replied that they were not, but that may have been a lie.

Princeton's highly advanced radar had been picking up mysterious objects for several days by then. The Navy called them "anomalous aerial vehicles," or AAVs—a term the military preferred to unidentified flying objects or UFOs, which had been tainted by its association with flying saucers, little green men, and countless crackpots.

According to Kevin Day, *Princeton*'s senior radar operator at the time, his screen showed over 100 AAVs over the course of the week. "Watching them on the display was like watching snow fall from the sky," he says in his first-ever on-camera interview for the History Channel's *Unidentified: Inside America's UFO Investigation* series.

Day claimed the AAVs appeared at an altitude greater than 80,000 feet, far higher than commercial or military jets typically fly. Initially, *Princeton*'s radar team didn't believe what they were seeing, chalking it up to anomalies and equipment malfunction. But after they determined that everything was operating as it should and they began detecting how the AAVs dropped with astounding speed to lower busier airspace, Day approached *Princeton*'s commander about taking action. "I was chomping at the bit," he says. "I just really wanted to intercept these things."

Two fighters were diverted to intercept one of the strange objects. When they first arrived on the scene, the pilots didn't see any flying objects. But they did observe what the lead pilot, Commander David Fravor later referred to it as a "disturbance" in the ocean. The water was churning with white waves breaking over what looked like a large object just beneath the ocean's surface.

Then they noticed one of the objects flying about 50 feet above the water. Fravor, the commander of the elite Black Aces squadron who was a Top Gun program graduate with more than 16 years of flying experience, described it as about 40 feet long, shaped like a Tic Tac breath mint, and with no obvious means of propulsion: "It's white. It has no wings. It has no rotors. I go, 'Holy sh*t, what is that?'"

Even odder were its swift and erratic movements that Fravor described as something he had never seen in his life. "This thing would go from one way to another, similar to if you threw a ping-pong ball against the wall."

Another Navy pilot who served as Fravor's wingman in the air that day spoke to the History Channel on the condition of anonymity. He gave an account very similar to Fravor's. Now a high-ranking Navy officer, she was a rookie pilot back in 2004. She remembered being terrified, watching as the more experienced pilots tried to intercept the strange craft. She stated, "It was so unpredictable—high G, rapid velocity, rapid acceleration. So, you're wondering: How can I possibly fight this?"

As Fravor flew around it, he says the craft ascended and came right at his plane: "All of a sudden it kind of turns and rapidly accelerates—beyond anything I've seen—crosses my nose, and...it's gone."

As the Tic Tac object accelerated into the distance, according to Day, Navy jets began launching off the carrier to try and intercept the other mysterious objects the Princeton's radar was tracking. While Fravor didn't capture the encounter on video, one of the pilots who took off after he landed was able to track it down. He managed to catch the video of a Tic Tac UFO, using a highly sensitive infrared camera.

Renewed attention to the Nimitz incident

While the *Nimitz* incident was known in naval circles and to some UFO/AAV buffs, it didn't get wide public attention until 2017, when *The New York Times* ran an article about the sighting, and released the video of the Tic Tac shot by the Nimitz pilot that day. The *Times* also revealed the existence of a little-known Defense Department initiative called the Advanced Aerospace Threat Identification Program, or AATIP. The "shadowy" enterprise, as the *Times* referred to it, had a budget of just $22 million, less than 0.004% of the department's total budget. It was said to be a pet project of then-Senate Majority Leader Harry Reid, who had a longtime interest in UFOs.

Although the government told the *Times* that AATIP had officially shut down in 2012, its former director, Luis Elizondo, insisted it was still operating. Elizondo left the program in October 2017, protesting that his work wasn't being taken seriously enough within the Defense Department. Elizondo has since joined *To the Stars Academy,* an organization co-founded by Tom DeLonge, best known as the guitarist with the band Blink-182. The group's mission included promoting UAP research.

According to Christopher Mellon, a former high-ranking U.S. intelligence official who is now a National Security Adviser to the organization, as well as numerous pilots, the Nimitz incident was not an isolated event. There have been more than a dozen incidents off the East Coast—some even more recent.

The Navy, which seemed to have made little effort to investigate the *Nimitz* episode back in 2004, also appears to be taking the subject more seriously now. Perhaps they were forced to investigate more pilots coming forward. By late April 2019, the Navy announced it was drafting new guidelines for reporting any sightings of "unidentified aircraft." The initiative was intended to de-stigmatize such reports and make it easier for service members to come forward with less fear of ridicule.

A Navy spokesman said, "There have been many reports of unauthorized and/or unidentified aircraft entering various military-controlled ranges and designated airspace in recent years." The Navy, it was announced, was "investigating each and every report."

As with all things UFO, AAV, and UAP, the *Nimitz* incident has its debunkers. Some have suggested the crafts were advanced reconnaissance drones and that the churning water was caused by a submarine. But whatever the now-famous Tic Tac was, it's hard to dispute that the pilots, the radar operators, and the infrared camera had seen something unknown.

Retired U.S. Navy Lieutenant Commander Alex Dietrich has found herself in the glare of media attention ahead of a highly anticipated government report on UFOs, a subject she says she has little interest in, despite encountering one on the job. "I don't consider myself a whistleblower. I don't identify as a UFO person," the former fighter pilot told Reuters in a Zoom interview, days before the report, expected to feature her own experience and dozens of others like it, was due for presentation to Congress.

During a routine training mission with the aircraft carrier USS Nimitz off the Southern California coast in November 2004, Dietrich and her then-commanding officer, fellow pilot David Fravor, was asked by another warship to investigate radar contacts in the area moving inexplicably. She also recounted they first noticed an unusual "churning" of the ocean surface before seeing what she and Fravor have described as a smooth, white oblong object resembling a large Tic Tac flying at high speed over the water.

When Fravor turned to "engage with" the object, "it appeared to respond in a way that we didn't recognize" because it seemed to lack "any visible flight control surfaces or means of propulsion," Dietrich recalled.

The U.S. Navy has previously confirmed the videos as authentic. Dietrich, now a mother of three, has discussed her experience in a recent joint appearance with Fravor on the CBS News program "60 Minutes," and has since addressed dozens of video calls from other journalists wanting to know more about her encounter in 2004.

Her answer remains the same as it has been for the past 17 years. "We don't know what it was, but it could have been a natural phenomenon in human activity. But the point was that it was weird, and we couldn't recognize it," Dietrich said.

Senior U.S. officials cited in the Times article said the report's ambiguity meant the government was unable to definitively rule out extraterrestrial origins of the sightings. The Times wrote that the U.S. intelligence in conjunction with the Pentagon covered more than 120 documented cases of enigmatic objects exhibiting speed and maneuverability exceeding known aviation technologies.

The USS Theodore Roosevelt UAP Incident

In 2015, Matthew Roberts was a US Naval service member stationed on the USS Theodore Roosevelt off the coast of West Florida. He sat down at his computer and watched in shock as a "Tic Tac" object was captured on radar doing extraordinary things that defied conventional aircraft capabilities. It gave him a sense of foreboding that he couldn't shake.

Later at the Office of Naval Intelligence, he discovered the truth of the UFO phenomenon and its implications for humanity. There are things today he still can't discuss from his 16 years in the Navy.

Roberts stated in an interview he's heard all kinds of things debunkers say and they haven't spent a day on a Naval ship. Debunkers claimed the Go-Fast event was a lock-on drone, but according to Robert, "These people have no idea what they are talking about. Pilots are highly trained, and they know what they are looking at on the radar.

"Some people believe it's our technology, but in the Roosevelt incident, that's not the case. No one was told anything," Roberts said, "We wouldn't put our military in a live-fire scenario with such important assets."

Nuclear Aircraft Carrier USS Theodore Roosevelt

In 2015, off the East Coast near the Florida coast, of the United States, an official U.S. Navy video of a UFO encounter was taken aboard a Navy fighter jet from the Nuclear Aircraft Carrier USS Theodore Roosevelt. One of the strange objects was spinning like a top against the wind and appeared almost daily from the summer of 2014 to March 2015, high in the skies over the East Coast.

Similar to the Nimitz reports, Navy pilots reported to their superiors that the objects had no visible engine or infrared exhaust plumes, but they reached 30,000 feet and hypersonic speeds.

"These things would be out there all day. Keeping an aircraft in the air requires a significant amount of energy. With the speeds we observed, 12 hours in the air is 11 hours longer than we'd expect," said Lt. Ryan Graves, a F/A-18 Super Hornet pilot who has been with the Navy for 10 years, and who reported his sightings to the Pentagon and Congress.

No one in the Defense Department has said that the objects were extraterrestrial, and experts emphasize that earthly explanations can be found for such incidents. Lieutenant Graves and four other Navy pilots, who said in interviews with The New York Times that they saw the objects in 2014 and 2015 in training maneuvers from Virginia to Florida off the aircraft carrier Theodore Roosevelt, make no such assertions of their origin.

Joseph Gradisher, a Navy spokesman, said the new guidance was an update of instructions that went out to the fleet in 2015, after the Roosevelt incidents. "There were a number of different reports," he said. Some cases could have been commercial drones, he said, but in other cases "We don't know who's doing this, we don't have enough data to track this. So, the message to the fleet intends to provide updated guidance on reporting procedures for suspected intrusions into our airspace."

Lieutenants Graves and Accoin spoke on the record to *The Times* about the objects. Three other pilots in the squadron also spoke to The Times about the objects but declined to be named. The pilots began noticing the objects after their 1980s-era radar was upgraded to a more advanced system. As one fighter jet after another got the new radar, pilots began picking up the objects, but ignoring what they thought were false radar tracks.

"People have seen strange stuff in military aircraft for decades," Lieutenant Graves said. "We're doing this very complex mission, to go from 30,000 feet, diving down. It would be a pretty big deal to have something up there." But he said the objects persisted, showing up at 30,000 feet, 20,000 feet, and even sea level. They could accelerate, slow down, and then hit hypersonic speeds.

Lieutenant Accoin said he interacted twice with the objects. The first time, after picking up the object on his radar, he set his plane to merge with it, flying 1,000 feet below it. He said he should have been able to see it with his helmet camera, but could not, even though his radar told him it was there.

A few days later, Lieutenant Accoin said a training missile on his jet locked on the object and his infrared camera picked it up as well. "I knew I had it, I knew it was not a false hit," he said. But still, "I could not pick it up visually."

At this point, the pilots said they speculated that the objects were part of some classified and extremely advanced drone program. But then pilots began seeing the objects. In late 2014, Lieutenant Graves said he was back at base in Virginia Beach when he encountered a squadron mate just back from a mission "with a look of shock on his face."

He said that he was stunned to hear the pilot's words. "I almost hit one of those things," the pilot told Lieutenant Graves.

The pilot and his wingman were flying in tandem about 100 feet apart over the Atlantic east of Virginia Beach when something flew between them, right past the cockpit. Lieutenant Graves said, 'It looked like a sphere encasing a cube.' The incident spooked the squadron so that an aviation flight safety report was filed, Lieutenant Graves said.

The near-miss according to Graves and other pilots interviewed, angered the squadron and convinced them that the objects were not part of a classified drone program. Government officials would know fighter pilots were training in the area, they reasoned, and would not send drones to get in the way.

"It turned from a potentially classified drone program to a safety issue," Lieutenant Graves said. "It was going to be a matter of time before someone had a midair" collision.

What was strange, the pilots said, was that the video showed objects accelerating to hypersonic speed, making sudden stops and instantaneous turns—something beyond the physical limits of a human crew. "Speed doesn't kill you," Lieutenant Graves said. "Stopping does. Or acceleration."

Asked what they thought the objects were, the pilots refused to speculate. "We have helicopters that can hover," Lieutenant Graves said. "We have aircraft that can fly at 30,000 feet and right at the surface." But "combine all that in one vehicle of some type with no jet engine, no exhaust plume."

Accoin added, "We're here to do a job, with excellence, not makeup myths."

In March 2015 the Roosevelt left the coast of Florida and headed to the Persian Gulf as part of the American-led mission fighting the Islamic State in Iraq and Syria. The same pilots who were interacting with the strange objects off the East Coast were soon doing bombing missions over Iraq and Syria. The incidents tapered off after they left the United States, the pilots said.

UFO Base of the Coast of Tulum, Yucatan

In Ardy Sixkiller Clarke's book, *Sky People, Untold Stories of Alien Encounters in Mesoamerica*, she traveled alone throughout Central America interviewing indigenous people about their remarkable Star People stories.

On the east coast of Mexico's Yucatan Peninsula sits the ancient Maya city, Tulum, meaning "city of dawn." The ruins overlook the Caribbean Sea. It was one of the last cities inhabited by the Mayas. This place has a history of UFO sightings. Among the indigenous people there, they talk about an underground station for UFOs.

The ancient city of Tulum has become a major tourist attraction with dancers, food courts, and lots of guides ready to take you on a sightseeing tour.

Dr. Clarke found an English-speaking guide named Geraldo, who for 300 pesos agreed to accompany her on a tour of the site.

Dr. Clarke questioned if he had seen UFOs and he replied, "Many times." He then described his UFO experience. "It was dusk. I was walking through the park with my friend who is a guard. He was checking to make sure there were no hiding tourists. They like to hide out so they can spend the night on the beach, but it is not allowed." He added that most Germans and Swedish tourists are disrespectful ones. Not gringos.

He continued, "My friend Ignacio and me were walking toward the exit when all of a sudden, the night turned to daylight. We looked upward and then toward the sea trying to locate the cause of the light. That's when we saw this huge craft that was shining a blinding orange light over the ocean. It cast this strange glow as far as you could see. The craft was just sitting there."

Geraldo said the craft remained stationary for two or three minutes and then dove into the sea and disappeared. He described them as fiery, orange balls before jet fighter planes arrived. He suggested to his friend Ignacio that they go to Mexico City and tell the soldiers what they had seen, but he said they wouldn't listen.

Then he surprised Dr. Clarke by saying, "I would tell them that the UFOs live under the sea. I do not know where they come from—maybe from space. Maybe they have always lived there, but whoever they are, the Mexican military chases them, and to me that makes them important."

Geraldo agreed with Dr. Clarke that they must have an undersea base where no one would bother them. "Perhaps they live in a world of water. Or maybe, a world with no water and they find the sea an interesting place to live."

Then he explained to Dr. Clarke that he had grown up in a small village nearby that was famous for the resistance during Yucatan's Caste War. He added that his mother's grandfather was part of the resistance and then he related another story that had taken place in the village.

"It was a dark night in the village. It had been raining and there were hurricane warnings. People were worried. The wind blew violently, and the rain poured down upon us. My family was thinking of leaving and going inland. It would be a difficult trek. We had no cars. Nothing but our feet. As my mother packed some food, a brilliant light flooded our small house. We all ran to the windows, seeking the source of the light. My grandmother yelled for us to get into the corner of the house for safety. I didn't obey. I ran out into the night and that is when I saw it.

"Overhead, just a tree-top level, there was a UFO. It was round, and it lit up the whole village. The rain stopped. The wind stopped. The UFO was like an umbrella. It was protecting us. For several hours the UFO stayed over our village. When the wind and rains lessened, it moved on. Some say it protected the village from flooding. Others gave reports of abduction. For me, I saw it, but I cannot explain it. I don't know if any of the stories were true."

When asked what the village elders said about the event, Geraldo replied, "They said the Sky Gods came back to protect us. They said our village survived because it was a reminder of the injustice visited upon the Maya people by the Mexican government. If it were destroyed, there would be no reminder."

Geraldo continued to talk about the time he observed a Star Traveler in the jungle one afternoon. He described the being that walked upright like a human, but it would drop down on all four feet and hands and run through the forest like a cat. He followed it as it changed colors and climbed trees like a monkey.

The being checked his surroundings, bent down, and pulled a long machine from under the forest trees. The machine was about three meters long and about a half meter wide (ten feet by two feet). Then the creature climbed inside the machine—a flying machine that made no noise.

Hidden from sight, Geraldo watched the flying machine for a few seconds, and then suddenly the machine began to spin and spin and slowly rose upward and, in a flash, it was gone. He wondered if he had observed what their holy men call a "shapeshifter."

A Shaman is believed to possess the ability to change their appearance, usually as animals, however, they never require a flying machine to travel.

Being superstitious and religious, Geraldo believed the alien brought him good luck. Shortly after his encounter with the Sky Man, he landed a good job.

U.S.S. Omaha encounter off the coast of San Diego

Leaked Pentagon footage of a spherical flying object sighted off the coast of San Diego shows a UFO soaring through the air before suddenly diving into the ocean. The footage was published on May 14 by documentary filmmaker Jeremy Corbell and was later confirmed as authentic by the Pentagon.

Buried within the thousands of pages of legislation under the "Committee Comments" section of the Intelligence Authorization Act for Fiscal Year 2021, a stipulation requested a report to senators on intelligence and armed services committees regarding any information surrounding UFO sightings and whether they present any potential threat.

While the exact nature of the purported extraterrestrial threats was unknown, former Director of National Intelligence John Ratcliffe has claimed, "there are a lot more sightings" than the public is aware of.

Ratcliffe said there have been objects observed by U.S. military craft and satellites that have achieved forms of flight that would normally be impossible with any known human technology. "When we talk about sightings, we are talking about objects that have been seen by Navy or Air Force pilots or have been picked up by satellite imagery that frankly engage in actions that are difficult to explain," he continued.

"Movements that are hard to replicate that we don't have the technology for. Or traveling at speeds that exceed the sound barrier without a sonic boom," Ratcliffe explained. The U.S. government declassified and released videos that show encounters between UFOs and U.S. Navy pilots in 2004 and 2015.

In September, the U.S. Navy acknowledged that videos showing the 2004 and 2015 UFO encounters by U.S. Navy pilots were released by former Blink-182 singer Tom DeLonge and published by The New York Times were of real "unidentified" objects.

"The Navy considers the phenomena contained/depicted in those three videos as unidentified," Navy spokesman Joseph Gradisher told *The Black Vault*, a website dedicated to declassified government documents. After the release of the videos, reports surfaced of a top-secret Pentagon program conducting classified briefings for more than a decade, analyzing various encounters between military craft and unidentified aerial vehicles.

In July, the Pentagon stated that the program was disbanded, but a Senate committee reported that they spent time on a program called the *Unidentified Aerial Phenomenon Task Force*. June 2020 U.S. Sen. Marco Rubio requested a detailed analysis on the findings of the task force. The reveal of both the task force's existence, as well as Rubio's data request, came in on June 17, 2020, Select Committee on Intelligence report authored by Rubio on the Intelligence Authorization Act.

Concerning Ratcliffe's comments on unexplained technology observed by U.S. military personnel and detailed in the upcoming report, at least one scientist can attest to having observed something similar.

Astrophysicist and former consultant for the UFO program since 2007, Eric W. Davis, told the New York Times in July 2020 that he gave a classified briefing to the Defense Department agency in March 2020 regarding "off-world vehicles not made on this Earth."

Chris Mellon, former Deputy Secretary of Defense said, "There seems to be a lot of continuity there, and unfortunately we just haven't been paying attention," said Chris Mellon, former Deputy Assistant Secretary of Defense for Intelligence. "What we are seeing is a number of distinct different things. Sometimes we're seeing a 50-foot object that can travel at hypersonic speeds and seemingly go into orbit or come down from altitudes above potentially 100,000 feet."

Russia's Lake Baikal for Underwater Aliens

Deep lakes throughout the world are rumored to have alien bases or portals entrances for their spacecraft. One such place is in southeastern Siberia, towards Mongolia's border, sits the planet's oldest and deepest lake. Nearly one-quarter of Earth's freshwater is contained there. Astonishing depths of over five thousand feet have been measured in certain areas. A myriad of unique plant and animal species inhabit the frigid territory, many of which exist nowhere else in the world. Scientists estimate this massive basin formed as an ancient rift valley more than twenty-five million years ago. For centuries, Lake Baikal has been home to a plethora of unexplained phenomena. Locals claim countless peculiar UFO encounters frequently occur within this remote region of Russia. Some theorize an extraterrestrial base is lurking beneath the lake's depths.

One of the most bizarre reports occurred in 1982 during a routine Soviet military training dive. While navigating the foreboding aquatic realm, Navy personnel noticed anomalous figures swimming nearby. Perplexed, they watched in bewilderment as several curious humanoid creatures approached them. Despite being stationed at a depth of over one hundred and sixty-four feet, these humanoids wore no modern equipment. Each donned a tight-fitting metallic suit complete with a helmet-like apparatus completely covering their heads and was estimated to be nine feet tall. Upon closer inspection, Navy troopers noticed the aliens were nearly ten feet tall. However, the colossal loch-dwellers soon disappeared back into the murky abyss.

Following this eerie run-in, the intrigued commander ordered his recruits to capture a subaqueous alien. Seven Scuba divers entered the glacial lake and began their harrowing descent. Soon after navigating an elevator of declining temperatures, multiple entities emerged. One frogman attempted to catch the unearthly specimen in a large net. At that moment, all hell broke loose for the unsuspecting group. Suddenly the nonhuman beings fought back by shooting intense sonar waves from strange devices, and a powerful force rendered every crew member unconscious, rapidly propelling them to the surface.

Catapulting upwards from extreme depths can have devastating effects on the body, resulting in a condition called "the bends." Three of the squadron were seriously injured but did not die due to this affliction. The remaining fellows needed immediate transfer to a decompression chamber. Unfortunately, there was only one decompression chamber in the region, and it was designed for merely two people at a time. Out of sheer desperation, four men entered simultaneously to save their lives. Tragically, this last-ditch effort did not go well. Three individuals perished because of their superior's hasty decision. Those who survived the terrifying ordeal were left with life-altering disabilities.

Following this harrowing catastrophe, KGB agents ceased further attempts to capture any USO (Unidentified Submerged Object) or humanoid creatures. For decades the horrifying events that transpired at Lake Baikal remained hidden by high-ranking authorities.

Vladimir Azhazha, a former Soviet Naval officer and esteemed ufologist, declared that Russian government executives recently released declassified files. In these documents, the Baikal aquanauts are described in detail. Predictably, Navy commanders had been extensively monitoring numerous underwater vehicles navigating the lake. Such technological capabilities greatly intrigued them—if engineers could replicate the vessels' inconceivable speeds, unprecedented militaristic advantages could be gained.

Throughout the eras, Lake Baikal has been no stranger to mysterious UFO activities. During the late 1950s, a TU-104 jet crashed into the lake after it was pursued by an unknown metallic vehicle. The frantic pilot radioed a distraught message to air traffic controllers informing them of this alleged attack. According to informants, all staff on duty at the time were forced to sign non-disclosure agreements. Numerous community fishermen attested to viewing the frightening aerial attack. Anglers described how a silver flying saucer chased a plane until it plummeted into the water and disappeared from their sight. Despite considerable testimonies, no conclusive evidence or official records of this event have ever surfaced.

In April 2009, the enigmatic Siberian sector made global headlines yet again. Astronauts aboard the International

Space Station photographed two circular convection breaks, thought to be produced by enormous aquatic crafts. One was located near the lake's center while the other was positioned towards Baikal's southern end. Both appeared to be created by something ascending beneath the thick ice-laden outer layer. The pair of disk-shaped cracks were perfectly symmetrical and astonishingly measured three miles in diameter. These immense fractures were so precise making them impossible to manufacture or replicate. Certain researchers believe the NASA-produced images are evidence of spaceships emerging from the dark waters below.

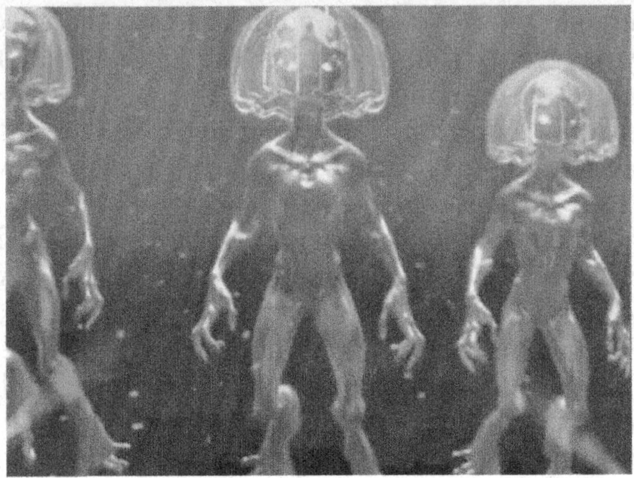

Artist's interpretation of Lake Baikal aliens

Oregon's Crater Lake and Alien Base

It was during the 1970s that my Los Angeles friend Roger had a bizarre UFO sighting over Crater Lake in Southern Oregon while flying his single-engine plane with a friend.

Roger was flying from Portland, Oregon to Los Angeles with a friend and decided to take a detour over Crater Lake. It was a clear day as he looked down on the placid lake and noticed a huge circular object either hovering above the water or sitting on it. Both he and his passenger were mesmerized by the image and at first, believed a large boat was sitting on the lake until the disc-shaped object suddenly dove into the water and continued to go straight down until it vanished beneath the water.

They knew that whatever they witnessed was not a boat.

Crater Lake is an ancient volcanic caldera situated in south-central Oregon in the western United States. It is the main feature of Crater Lake National Park and is famous for its deep blue color and water clarity. It is one of the world's deepest lakes, 1,949 feet deep, and is the deepest lake in the United States. Like Russia's Lake Baikal, Crater Lake is enchanting, but the lake holds a deadly secret—a large number of people have died there under mysterious circumstances or completely vanished there.

The long history of volcanic activity at Crater Lake suggests that this volcano may erupt again someday. The most recent eruption occurred on the lake floor in the western part of the caldera in 1945, where bubbling gases were released.

Hot springs and fumaroles (geothermal vents of natural gases) surround the crater rim, and studies indicate there is still lingering hydrothermal activity taking place in the depths of the lake. The cataclysmic eruption that collapsed the volcanic mountain and created a caldera is believed to have happened as recently as 4600 BC.

The lake is rumored to have a sea monster and a large number of Bigfoot reports. Park Rangers once reported following a large, dark, putrid-smelling creature through the woods until it started throwing pinecones at them. Two deaths supposedly occurred at the park and were attributed to Bigfoot, but the bodies were quickly whisked away by government agents.

Stories of hauntings, UFOs, and mysterious campfires continue to this day that seemed to ignite by themselves on the lake's Wizard Island. One of the strangest stories is about the Old Man of the Lake, a tree stump, probably hemlock, that has been floating vertically in Crater Lake since 1896. The stump, sun-bleached and bone-white, has baffled park officials for years because it not only bobs in the water but can travel four miles in one day and is also buoyant enough to support the weight of a person standing on top of it.

Investigator John Salinas offered a possible explanation for the Old Man's physics-defying behavior when the Old Man stump slipped into the lake, he had rocks bound within his roots. However, this theory doesn't hold water (no pun intended) because not one rock has been found under it.

The Klamath, Modoc, Yahooskin, and other Indian tribes have called the Klamath Basin home for over ten thousand years. In 1853, the Europeans discovered the lake by accident as they were seeking gold. There are many myths, but Barbara Alatorre, a Klamath Tribal Member and historian, tells of her people's story as the place of creation. "Before time began, giant Spirit Being came down to earth through a hole in the sky, pushing ice down to build giant mountains.

"The first mountain built by the Klamath Spirit Beings was *Moy Yaina* (Big Mountain where Mt. Mazama currently stands). The Spirit Beings created the rest of the Klamath terrain by digging tunnel-like caverns beneath the Earth, and by pushing up the hills and mountains to create the Cascade Range. They dug the channels for rivers and created marshes and hundreds of springs that bubble up from the underground. Giant trees, meadows, and plants sprung up everywhere.

"Upon completion, all the Spirits returned to the afterworld (called Nolis-Gaeni), where others may not go until after death. Only the Spirit Chief, Skell (the Sky Creator), remained behind to create human beings (*maqlags*).

"Skell made his home inside Mt. Shasta (*Mlaiksi*) at the southern end of the *maqlaqs* country. From his spirit bag, Skell selected two bones as he soared over to what is now Klamath Lake where he laid the bones over one another—(giving birth to the Klamaths). Two bones were crossed near Modockni Lake known today as Tule Lake (home of the Modocs). Finally, near Goose Lake, bones were laid together (to become progenitors of the Yahooskin and Wal-pah-pe people).

"The Klamath tale goes on to describe Llao, the Chief of the Underworld, who would occasionally come up to the surface and observe the humans living in their splendid realm. Once during one of his spying sessions, he saw Loha who was the daughter of a Klamath chief. Loha was exceptionally beautiful and refused all suitors which included all the bravest warriors from the surrounding clans.

"During an important ceremonial observance, Llao sent his supernatural entourage to entice Loha and they dispatched her suitors in a blast of orange light. The extravagant gifts, the suspicious nature of the entourage, and their otherworldly removal of the suitors overwhelmed Loha with fear.

"She reported what she had experienced to her father, and he and the elders decided to hide her so that Llao could not force her to live inside the mountain with him as his wife. The tradition then says, that when Llao returned and could not find Loha, and nobody would reveal her whereabouts, he flew into a rage, wreaking havoc beneath the crater in the subterranean realm causing volcanic activity to ravage the people out of revenge.

"Two powerful medicine men sought to evoke Skell, their benevolent creator, to rescue the people from the wrath of Llao, so they walked by torchlight up to the rim and sacrificed themselves to the underworld."

There seems to be a common theme from Native Americans about beings that created the world from the sky and return to the underworld. Do those beings still reside beneath the Lake?

People who Vanish at Crater Lake

This story took place on July 4, 1947. According to the Crater Lake Foundation, Mr. Cornelius and his wife were on vacation at Crater Lake, when suddenly, Mr. Cornelius handed his wallet to his wife and then spontaneously slid down a rock chute. He was injured from the fall, but still alive, and then he hobbled into the lake and drowned himself.

There was no motive or signs that Cornelius was suicidal.

The next story happened in October of 2006 when Kenneth Boehlke and his eight-year-old son Sammy were staying at Diamond Lake and decided to visit Crater Lake. They stopped in a parking lot near Cleetwood Cove where

Sammy proceeded to get out and play hide and seek as they liked to do. Sammy went near a large boulder formation and down the adjacent hill, but his father Kenneth lost sight of him. When he reached the top of the hill, Sammy was gone.

A massive search began for Sammy involving two hundred searchers, helicopters, and K-9-unit dogs, that lasted for months. No trace of Sammy was ever found. Even the FBI was involved in the search, but it was unusual that they were involved. The FBI's criteria do not involve lost children in the forests.

Another place known for mysterious disappearances is the vast cave system at the Oregon Caves National Monument.

Lake Tahoe Disappearances

Lake Tahoe, a freshwater lake, is 1,644 feet deep. Like Crater Lake, UFOs have been spotted entering and exiting the water on numerous occasions. There are also plenty of missing people and children reports—and the theories suggest some have drowned while the other missing people are never found.

David Paulides, the author of the *411 Missing* series of books, has written about large number chilling disappearances at national parks including Lake Tahoe.

What confounds investigators about many of these cases is that dogs used to pick up the scent of the missing person can't locate them. Often, the search dogs go in circles as if the person was airlifted from a certain spot on the ground, never to be seen again.

Dawn Raimond, a 41-year-old resident of Round Hill, noticed something odd in the sky over Lake Tahoe from the deck of her home one evening. According to Dawn, she was sitting outside on her deck at about 11:40 p.m. looking at the stars, when she noticed moving lights in the sky, but then the stars started moving.

The lights were arranged straight up and down and then spreading out. Dawn called out to her daughter, Raven, 20, to come outside and witness the strange lights. As the lights came closer to their house, the two women were able to see the strange object with two lights.

"It wasn't an airplane," Raven said.

What they saw was a dark, triangle-shaped object traveling fast across the lake toward their home, and then it slowed down as it approached her house, according to Dawn Raimond. The object was completely silent but moved within 500 feet of their house. When it came to a stop above the trees, the lights began to get wider and wider and then started fading.

"It disappeared right in front of our eyes," Dawn said. She's convinced it wasn't an airplane or an airplane from the Naval Air Station in Fallon, or a stealth fighter. "I know what they look like and (there's) no way it was that. It was much bigger than that."

The Raimonds' sighting comes just over a year after another Lake Tahoe resident, Allan Brown, saw and videotaped a UFO over Lake Tahoe reported on June 16, 2006, in the Tahoe Daily Tribune. Brown was able to videotape an object "dancing in the sky" over the lake in the early morning hours.

CHAPTER NINE

The Vanished

Over 16,000 people have vanished in Alaska since 1988 and not a trace of them has been found. It is as if they walked into another dimension.

The following stories come from the Travel Channel's, *The Alaska Triangle,* which had some of the spookiest true stories of anomalies and missing people in the triangle. UFOs sightings take place over Ketchikan, Skagway, and Sitka, Alaska. Nome is another eerie place where people seem to vanish in thin air.

Nome, Alaska 2005: Brian Kulik, an Indigenous Alaskan, had two family members vanish. One family member rode out into the snow alone on his snowmobile one day and never returned. His snowmobile was found but what was baffling about it was the snowmobile track ended at a certain point and his relative's footprints were nowhere around the snowmobile. Search teams looked for him but found nothing.

Was he beamed aboard a UFO or did he walk into a portal?

Brian Kulik had his own sinister encounter with a UFO one night while driving near Teller, Alaska, 2 miles from Nome. Suddenly, he noticed a strange saucer-shaped object in the sky, round and polished, following him. It hovered above him and beamed a brilliant light on him, making it impossible to see. That's all he remembered as the UFO shot into the sky.

Marathon Man vanishes without a trace

On July 4, 2012, an Anchorage man named Michael LeMaitre went missing as he competed in Mount Marathon, a grueling Seward footrace typically held on the Fourth of July each year. He was never seen again. LeMaitre was running Mount Marathon for the first time. It was especially rainy, foggy, and slick that day.

The 66-year-old businessman and grandfather were last seen about three hours into the race, climbing just shy of the race's turnaround point at an elevation of about 3,000 feet. LeMaitre never came down. An extensive search turned up nothing.

"No clues. No trace. No trail," an Alaska State Troopers spokeswoman said at the time. LeMaitre's story attracted widespread media attention, becoming one of the most well-known in a grimly extensive list of Alaskans who've disappeared into wilderness landscapes without a trace. His disappearance was especially striking because he had been participating in an event that each year draws tens of thousands of spectators to Seward, and hundreds of runners onto the mountain itself. "The mountain swallowed this man," a relative told Runner's World journalist Christopher Solomon for an extensive article about the case in 2016.

After troopers stopped their search, the family continued. LeMaitre was declared legally dead in October 2012 after a court proceeding known as a presumed death trial. His wife sued the race and the Seward Chamber of Commerce for $5 million, alleging negligence and emotional distress. In 2014, the Seward Chamber of Commerce settled with the family for a payment of $25,000. Calls to her for this story went unanswered.

LeMaitre's disappearance changed the way the race operates. New rules were instituted, including one that says runners now must sign a pledge saying they've completed the roughly 3-mile racecourse at least once before race day. Participants who don't make it to a halfway point within one hour are disqualified, and race sweepers now follow the last runner to the top of the mountain and back down, said race director Matias Saari.

Though declared legally dead for about nine years, LeMaitre is still considered a missing person by Alaska State Troopers. Being declared dead by the court system doesn't remove someone from the state missing persons clearinghouse, said Austin McDaniel, a spokesman for the troopers. "Law enforcement has to place eyes on him, alive and well," McDaniel said. "Or remains need to be found."

A partial human jawbone was found near Tonsina Point, a few mountainous miles away, in 2014. There as speculations whether the remains belonged to LeMaitre, but DNA testing found they instead belonged to a 39-year-old man whose last address was in Arkansas, troopers said. Other remains associated with the man were found in the same area in 1997, according to troopers.

Nothing of LeMaitre has ever been found.

CHAPTER TEN

Mystery at the Seismic Station

It was in October of 2015 that seismic activity equipment detected a large disturbance before cutting out at the Kultieth River Mountain station in southeast Alaska even though there was no tectonic activity in the area at the time. The shaking detected by the station lasted for at least eight minutes before the transmission stopped.

The Alaska Earthquakes Center seismic sensor recorded the increased activity. Field engineer Scott Dalton made this very strange comment, "The data indicated it was something big moving out there before the data stopped coming in."

Scientists wondered if some huge beast was outside the remote seismic station after the recording equipment was triggered and then wiped out even though there was no earthquake. Even stranger was when the scientific team investigated the area, they found teeth marks on the lids of containers that hold the equipment.

They wondered if a bear was responsible for the damage.

According to Bruce Schneider, an ancient mammoth tusk hunter who gathers relic tusks through Alaska where the great mammoths once roamed 10,000 years ago before the glaciers, a population of 3-meter-tall dwarf mammoths survived on Russia's Wrangel Island until 3,700 years ago. In the early 1900s, an article appeared in an Alaskan newspaper that frozen prints of mammoths were found.

Legends by Alaskan natives say they were hunting the woolly mammoth two centuries ago. Is it possible a number of the giants that stood fourteen feet tall didn't go extinct?

Kultieth River Mountain station in Southeast Alaska

Alaska's Jurassic Park

Every kind of conceivable creature exists in Alaska according to eyewitnesses and indigenous legends—giant humans, Big Foot aka Sasquatch, little people, and even extinct dinosaurs like the Pterodactyl and Plesiosaur reside in Alaska's lakes.

The remote Lake Iliamna claims to have its own Lochness Scotland monster. Witnesses described the huge lake monster as having a long neck and two or three humps on its back. Reports of a monster living in the Lake came from the Native Tlingit people, who called it *Gonakedet*. They described it as a water serpent with a head and tail similar to a wolf, and a body like an orca whale. It was believed to be a "Fish God" to the native people and its existence was recorded in pictographs along the Alaskan and British Columbian coasts.

The Aleut people also passed on legends of the creature they called Jig-ik-nak. The monsters were reported to travel in groups and attack canoes and kill warriors.

Through the years, the sightings continued, especially small planes flying over the lake just to glimpse the monster. In 1979, the anchorage daily news, the state's main newspaper, offered a reward of $100,000 to anyone who offer proof of the lake monster's existence. So far, no one has been able to claim the reward money.

In 1967, Alaska Missionary Chuck Crapuchettes has seen the monster twice. Once, he was flying over in a floatplane and he saw a large creature swimming in the water. He tried to radio other people around the area to verify it, but nobody got there in time.

One of his friends went trolling for the monster. He took a 5/16 stainless steel cable, put #2 tuna hooks on it, baited them with caribou, and tied it off on the struts of his floatplane. While he was drifting and sitting out on the floats his plane suddenly gave a big jerk and knocked him off the floats. The plane was being towed off and he barely made it to shore. He walked for miles while the plane was towed around the lake. When he finally recovered his airplane, three of the cables were gone. Some of the tuna hooks, eight to nine inches long, were straightened out!

Lake Iliamna is 80 miles long, the largest lake in Alaska, and one-thousand feet deep. Some believe that the monster is a rare population of freshwater harbor seals that scientists believed traveled from the ocean eons ago. Cryptozoologists suggest the 20' foot or larger creature is the extinct dinosaur Plesiosaur, which populated lakes millions of years ago and its ancestors survived for eons eating an abundance of salmon. Like Lake Iliamna, Scotland's Loch Ness Lake contains salmon, and this monster seems to enjoy a fish diet.

Many people have reported their propellers damaged by what looks like teeth marks. Those teeth marks are explained away by the white sturgeon fish, a bottom dweller, that rarely surfaced and has a touch armor skin. It's doubtful that it was a sturgeon. This fish is not known to have long necks, or long tails that undulate on the water surface like a snake.

Robin, a Native Elder, believes that the lake is linked to the ocean through deep cracks and fissures. But the lake isn't the only place where monsters have been seen.

Something very large lurks in the water of the Chena River in Fairbanks, Alaska. In 2016, two employees of the Alaskan Bureau of Land Management, Craig McCaa and Ryan Delaney caught whatever it was on video. They estimated it was 12' or 15' feet long.

The Bureau of Land Management posted a mysterious film on Facebook at the end of October 2016. "Our Fairbanks employees captured this strange 'thing,' swimming in the Chena River," the post read. It moved like a snake in the water and had ice on its back. It was dubbed "The Alaskan Ice Monster. Theories suggested it was a massive sturgeon, a zombie salmon, a shark, a scabby whale, a pet alligator, an icy moose hide, an arthropod, or a giant Arctic crocodile. Some observers noticed it had tentacles and gills.

It appears that Alaska is a portal or stargate for everything imaginable. We are left to wonder if extraterrestrials or otherworldly beings abduct humans in Alaska for experimentation like the ongoing cattle mutilations. People don't just vanish into thin air. Of course, there are logical explanations for some of the missing people, but there are cases that continue to baffle investigators.

Is there a secret black triangle base hidden inside Mount Hayes where UFOs appear and disappear as if entering a portal and is the base used to create new life forms, where aliens and U.S. military side by side?

CHAPTER ELEVEN

Alaska's Giant Cannibals

This is a mosquito original story from the Tlingit people of Southeast Alaska, who live in Klukwan, on the Chilkat River. Many years ago, on the mountain above Klukwan lived a giant. The giant would come down into the fish camp and steal the salmon from the drying racks. This angered the villagers and made them thin and hungry. When the fish were gone, the giant began hunting and killing the villagers for food. It killed and ate many people. They were afraid to leave their homes and fearful for their children. They tried to kill it with spears, but the spears just bounced off the giant's thick skin.

The villagers called a council to decide how to get rid of the giant. They tracked the giant up the mountain, and into the woods. Soon they saw a large community house with blood-red smoke rising from the chimney. They knew this was the cannibal's home. They decided to build a trap like the hunters do for grizzly bears. They dug a deep pit and lined the bottom with a tough sinew net. The hole was very deep, deeper than for a grizzly bear, and they covered it with branches and twigs to match the forest floor. Early in the morning, the villagers sent a fast and light hunter to the giant's home to draw the enemy out. The hunter, chased by the cannibal, ran lightly over the top of the trap. The heavy giant crashed through the poles and branches and snared himself in the net at the bottom. The villagers filled the pit with wood and soaked it with fish oil. When they brought the torches, the cannibal realized what they intended. He roared out that they did not have the power to kill him and even burned to ash he would feed on them.

To stop the cannibal from keeping his promise, the villagers kept the fire burning for four days and four nights. On the fifth day, the fire had burned down to ashes. The villagers took a long pole and stirred the ashes to make sure nothing remained of the giant. As they stirred, ashes and sparks flew into the air and changed into mosquitoes that dived at once, biting and feeding on the villagers' blood. The cannibal giant's promise was fulfilled, and he returns today to feed on the blood of people.

Lovelock Giants

Throughout the West and in Alaska indigenous people have handed down oral stories of the giants. In Nevada, the Paiutes described them as red-headed giants. These fearsome cannibals threatened the Paiute people and other Native American tribes until one day, they banded together to defeat their enemies at Lovelock Cave.

On May 24, 1984, Lovelock Cave went on the National Register of Historic Places. The dry conditions rather than the typical moist conditions of most caves make this cave particularly conducive to preservation. This meant organic and inorganic materials from long ago were here. Ancient peoples lived in this cave for 4,000 years, and the artifacts recovered shed some light on their culture and life in the Great Basin.

Humboldt Sink, Lovelock Cave's location, is a valley that was once completely under Lake Lahontan. Also known as Bat Cave, Horseshoe Cave, Sunset Guano Cave, and Indian Cave, Lovelock Cave is 20 miles south of Lovelock, Nev., near the Humboldt State Wildlife Management Area.

In 1886, the Paiutes told a local mining engineer about the cave and took him to the site to prove its existence. He couldn't get an archeological excavation underway, but in 1911, two miners started digging out guano, bird, and bat excrement, which is a perfect fertilizer. However, they had no interest in using the guano for fertilizer; they wanted to use it for gunpowder. During their excavation, the two miners contacted Alfred Kroeber, founder of the University of California Anthropology Department, when they discovered artifacts inside the cave. The first true archaeological dig started in 1912. A second dig took place in 1924.

When the report was finally released, about 10,000 artifacts were found, from tools to bones to weapons. Duck decoys—with features still attached, making them the oldest known duck decoys in the world. Radiocarbon dating found human bones dating back to 1450 BC.

Were giant skeleton bones found in Lovelock Cave? Mummified remains of a man who was over six feet tall were found in Lovelock Cave. Additionally, the researchers discovered a 15-inch sandal. As with all sensational discoveries, controversies, debates, legends, and conspiracies followed. Media personnel and entrepreneurs looking to establish a tourist attraction or make a name for themselves and grabbed this news story. They created a narrative about red-haired cannibalistic giants. However, the story isn't as off-base as it seems.

In the book, *Fossil Legends of the First Americans*, Adrienne Mayor discussed the oral traditions of Native Americans and the stories they have accepted into their culture. The Paiute legend of the red-haired giants is one of those stories. Sarah Winnemucca Hopkins, daughter of a

Paiute Indian chief, wrote about this legend her ancestors passed down in 1882.

Mayor explains in her book that these skeletal remains were within 100 miles of fossils of much larger creatures like mammoths and bears. The assumption that these were giants could easily have been made by untrained, everyday people. She also explains that hair pigment doesn't remain after death. However, the conditions within Lovelock Cave could have turned dark hair a reddish color, so the claim isn't that far-fetched. The Paiute people have a story passed down from generation to generation. The *Si-Te-Cah* or Sai'i is a legendary tribe of vicious, cannibalistic red-haired giants.

As mentioned above, Sarah Winnemucca Hopkins wrote down this oral tradition in 1882. In her book, she detailed a great battle that led to their deaths at what is now Lovelock Cave. Si-Te-Cah means "tule eaters," which refers to a plant the giants used to make rafts to escape the Paiutes.

Lake Lahontan was an ancient lake in the area. The legend explains how all tribes came together to defeat these red-haired giants. After backing them into a cave, the Paiutes started a fire at its entrance. The Si-Te-Cah, who didn't try to escape, burned alive or suffocated, while tribe members killed any deserters leaving the cave. In addition to the duck decoys, the 15-inch sandal, and human remains, the archeological digs found an incredible assortment of items that give us a glimpse into life thousands of years ago. Excavators found woven basket fragments, stone smoke pipes, shells, an antique duck call, and more.

The remains found indicate that humans were above average for that period. Considering the average height of an American man today is 5 feet 9 inches, it's not hard to imagine why the Paiute people thought a group of men over six feet tall were giants.

There are stories of giants in the Bible, and there are stories of giant skeletons unearthed in the Mounds of Ohio. In the late 1800s, John Everhart published an account of these sensational discoveries in his "History of Muskingum County," expecting that it would boost sales of the book. He included a letter signed by several participants stating that nine giant skeletons had been found ranging in size from 8 to 9½ feet tall "by actual measurement." Another member of the crew eventually admitted, however, that "all the skeletons were so much crumbled that it was difficult to make accurate measurements."

One of the objects recovered from the mound was a sandstone slab with several circular depressions that might have been used for cracking nuts. Two months after the stone was unearthed, Everhart announced that it also was inscribed with hieroglyphics —"chiefly Greek, commingled with Phoenician and Etruscan." As if that wasn't amazing enough, he also claimed that the stone was buried alongside an 8-foot-tall skeleton. However, he never paid his workmen, and one of them took him to court, where another testified that he'd never been paid the $15 he'd been promised to carve the inscription on the slab and give it "the appearance of ancient work." So, the supposedly ancient inscription was a deliberate fraud.

Was there any giant skeleton found? Everhart's book included a letter signed by several participants stating that nine giant skeletons had been found ranging in size from 8 to 9 ½ feet tall "by actual measurement." Another member of the crew eventually admitted that "all the skeletons were so much crumbled that it was difficult to make accurate measurements."

If you do a Google search for giant skeletons in the Smithsonian Museum, you will find tons of debunking articles and YouTube videos. No surprise our government doesn't want the truth out that giants roamed Earth, and they might have been extraterrestrials.

If the Bible mentions giants, they must have existed eons ago. Giants are mentioned in the Bible in several places:
Genesis 6:4; Joshua 12:4, Og, King of Basham in Deuteronomy 3:11; the giant people in Canaan that Moses' spies reported in Numbers 13:30-33; Goliath and David in Samuel 21:19; and the Anankites in Deuteronomy 9:1-2.

CHAPTER TWELVE

Sasquatch in Alaska

There's an elusive hairy beast known by Indigenous people throughout the world as Bigfoot, Sasquatch, Yeti, Almas, Yowie, Didi, Skookum, Seatco, Skunk Ape, Misaabe, Bush Men, and Dooligah. Some believe these creatures are emissaries between our world and the underworld, and they possess supernatural powers and telepathic qualities to avoid capture by humans.

For generations, the Suqpiag people of the Nanwalek and Port Graham area have told stories of a mysterious being, Nantinaq, that lurks in the thick forests of the southern Kenai Peninsula, especially the Port Chatham area. Tales have been handed down of a large hairy being, like Bigfoot, that uproots trees, makes mysterious knocking sounds, and sometimes causes people to disappear. Could Nantinaq be the elusive Big Foot creatures seen throughout the Northwest?

For 40 days in late spring and early summer, a team of five – Ash Naderhoff, Keith Seville, Noah Craig, DJ Brewster, and Kyle McDowell – camped out in the Port Chatham area looking for Nantinaq. With a video crew, they explored the area, setting up game cameras and taking audio recordings – very spooky and weird recordings. The series includes interviews with a historian, Jeff Davis, local elders, and a psychic, Polly Wyrum. Parts of the show also were filmed in Homer and Nanwalek.

The last covc on the peninsula heading south before Chugach Passage and the Chugach Islands, Port Chatham includes the abandoned village of Portlock. At the head of Port Chatham is a little side cove, Chrome Bay, its name referencing a mid-19th century chrome mine. All private property, the area belongs mostly to the English Bay Corporation and includes some Alaska Native allotments.

Seventy years ago, residents abandoned the area, some say because of the terrifying presence of Nantinaq. The stories of Port Chatham have been the subject of numerous magazine articles and a recent book by local author Larry Baxter, *Abandoned: The History and Horror of Port Chatham.* Back in the 1970s, Evans said a man claimed to have been abducted for five days by something. His wife got suspicious and suspected he might have been messing around with a woman in another village. The man said he couldn't talk about what happened, but his wife antagonized him so much that he talked.

"He told and died," Evans said. "His hair fell out and he turned purple."

One time while working on the Exxon Valdez Oil Spill in 1989, Evans said he stayed at a cabin on Port Chatham.

"I saw some crazy stuff that happened," he said. "Weird sounds, just stuff happening around the cabin that kept us on our haunches."

That's a common theme of the Nantinaq stories: strange knocking sounds coming from the woods.

"There was this one incident. We were out kind of late," Evans said. "We were outside and talking. It was kind of crazy.

It sounded like whatever was listening to us was mimicking our conversation."

In a clip from the series on the show's Facebook page, Naderhoff and the team are shown listening to one of those strange sounds. They're setting up a game camera and cutting away branches with an axe. From the woods, they hear sounds like an axe chopping wood. He said the knocking went on for 15 minutes, though only a few minutes are shown in the series. Naderhoff said they would make knocking sounds, varying the pattern, and something in the woods repeated it.

"You just change it up a little, it would come back the exact same," he said. "I believe that's the first time we made contact with something was right there."

Evans said stories continue about Nantinaq in Nanwalek. "One thing we've noticed is our dogs react different," he said. "If there's a bear in the vicinity, they're not so scared. ... If there's another thing, they're going to hide. They're going to try to come inside the house."

Kniffel said he thinks there's more material to do a show beyond the eight episodes. "There's still plenty to explore. We found a ton of stuff out there, bizarre stuff nobody expected," he said. "I have the feeling we've just scratched the surface."

Even with just the first two episodes broadcast, Naderhoff said he's already experienced a bit of reality TV fame. He visited Soldotna recently and went to a restaurant with his wife to eat. At 6-foot 6-inches tall with his long, salt-and-pepper beard and blue beanie hat, Naderhoff is recognizable.

"I took three steps in the door. It was 'Ash,'" he said, as people he didn't know called him by name. "Even going to the laundromat now, people find you talking. It wasn't something I expected."

Naderhoff said he hopes the Discovery Channel's *Alaskan Killer Bigfoot* will bring some exposure to Nanwalek and to Homer. Evans said he's heard a lot of positive feedback in Nanwalek about *Alaskan Killer Bigfoot*.

"I think besides being oral history amongst the people, I think it's a story that needs to be shared so we don't make the same mistake," he said "We talk about history repeating itself.

We don't want to send people down and find out it's something else."

The 1967 photo above was a video taken by Roger Patterson and his friend Bob Gimlin of Big Foot near Bluff Creek in Northern California. They said the creature was 7 1/2 feet tall. Professor of Anatomy and Anthropology Jeff Meldrum analyzed the video and has shown it to his classes at the Department of Biological Sciences at Idaho State University. He said it shows muscular area in the back that could not be a human in an ape suit. This is one of the clearest videos ever taken of Big Foot.

Sasquatch Revelation

In the book, *The Sasquatch Message to Humanity*, by SunBow, he explains that a Sasquatch has communicated with him since May 2015 on Vancouver Island. One night he conducted ceremonies and chants that echoed in the mountains around Kennedy Lake. Soon after on another night, he heard a loud bang that sounded as if a big tree trunk was hit on a hollow tree.

Cryptologists who have studied the behavior of Sasquatch believe they mark their territory by pulling up large trees by the roots. Giant footprints, hair samples, videos of the creature, and their spine-tingling howl have been recorded over the years.

Trees began to shake and then SunBow heard footsteps and knew Sasquatch wanted to meet him. Telepathically, he said to the giant creature, "We are relatives. I come to meet you as a brother, to learn of who you are. Maybe you can help me understand why sad stories have happened between your people and mine. And maybe we can help in healing our collective past."

The Sasquatch replied telepathically, "You heard our call and you came. I heard your call and I came. I am an elder seer of my people sent to meet and teach you. I haven't met any of your people who can talk with us in a few of your generations. My and your people used to be close brothers, living side by side, in the early ages of your Human species, when you could still sit in the Council of the Star Elders. We were your elder brother protecting and teaching you. We helped your species to learn, grow and adapt to this home planet where you were created, on which we had been living since long before your conception.

"Our people, like yours, were bioengineered by the Star Elders, but we were born many eons before you were. Our conceptors added to their alien genetics the DNA of the most evolved and adapted species of that era—a giant lemur (believed to be the size of a gorilla), now long extinct, just like they did to create your species much later with the DNA of another evolved large primate that you call Anthropopithecus. This is why our genetics and yours are so closely related that our species can interbreed. This is also why your species and ours are the only two having spliced genes in this home planet. So, we come from the same star seeds, making us relatives, but our earthly ancestors are different. So, we are not your ancestors, but your elder brothers.

"My people were created as part of a cosmic plan to allow ancient souls of star beings to incarnate on this young planet and help it evolve into an intergalactic outpost of consciousness while discovering its man resources and life forms. We were conceived to possess mighty physical strength and resistance with thick skin and fur to adapt to every possible environment and climate, from now-capped summits to dense jungles, and to be protected from mosquito and snake bites. My people also have strong limbs that enable us to break trees, run fast, and jump high and far; keen eyesight and clairvoyance to see in the darkness even in the deepest caves of the underworld, huge lungs to swim underwater over long distances and be perfectly autonomous and self-sufficient without need for any external material support.

"We were also gifted with powerful psychic abilities that we have kept to this day including telepathy, mind reading, remote viewing, hypnosis, astral projection, dematerialization, teleportation, shape-shifting, and permeating consciousness. This last ability allows us to impregnate an area and surround entities with our soul. So, we might be perceived as interdimensional beings, but in reality, we are an incarnated species with highly developed psychic powers like none other from this home planet.

"Your first ancestors too were created with those same psychic abilities, but your evolutionary course has largely depleted your gifts as well as your longevity. We have kept our connection with the great Soul of our species like most animals have, while our telepathic abilities allow the average individual among us to tap in and communicate from distances with any other one gifted with this faculty. So, any one of us can know any time how any other thinks and feels, through telepathy. When one connects with our greater Soul, the whole species can potentially know about it. But our individualities remain independent and free, so individual behaviors are not always representative of our great Soul species.

"Likewise, we can read the minds and intentions of others. That's why those fools who chase us like beasts, with guns and infrared glasses, will never catch a glimpse of any of us. Our telepathic abilities allow us to foresee who is coming and feel their intentions. So, we can hardly ever be surprised by one of yours, except maybe when we are deeply asleep or when one of your fast-moving vehicles comes our way. Otherwise, we ourselves to your people only to frighten away some unwelcome intruders, or in the rare cases when one of you is willing and able to communicate peacefully in spirit with us.

"Once one of you has established contact with our greater Soul, we can always communicate in spirit afterward, regardless of distances, much like we do with our Star Elders.

"As we are incarnated beings, there are plenty of physical proofs of our existence, but we usually conceal most traces and offer proper burial to our dead in undisclosed protected locations, inaccessible to your species. Some of your people go around hunting us either to find or to cover up physical proof of our existence and they have succeeded in doing both. Being highly telepathic beings, when some of you identify tracks left by one of us, that one of ours knows who it is and what their intention is.

"Likewise, when one of yours succeeds in taking pictures of one of ours and publishes them, we can hear the thoughts of those seeing it and feel the fears, hatred, and ridicule we are subjected to in the uncivilization enslaving your people. This hurts our Soul. For this reason, we avoid cameras and having our DNA sampled. Material proofs of our existence can also threaten the safety of my people, if used to track us by the powers serving the lower lords, including some of your people, knowingly or not.

"Our human allies are not concerned about proving our physical existence since there will always be denial in the uncivilization of the lower lords, no matter how much evidence is provided, to maintain the official program of the global control agenda through the false doctrine of speciesism and an ideology of domination. Our Human allies are concerned about our rehabilitation in your collective consciousness as your elder relatives and long-time allies, through the transmission of the ancient knowledge we have carried to this day that has largely been forgotten by your people so that we can once again as before work together in reestablishing the Divine Law and Cosmic Order on our home planet.

"Some of us still live thousands of years and see your earthly kingdoms come and go, like leaves on trees throughout the seasons, what your first ancestors could achieve when you were sitting with the immortals in the Star Council (Methuselah lived to be 969 years old according to the Old Testament). But your people were later subdued under the control of the rebellious lower lords and modified to be more easily submitted. You were bioengineered to be dependent and vulnerable, needing external material support for your basic survival, like clothing, shoes, fire, shelter, tools, or weapons that my people don't need to roam wild and free in every kind of environment. This vulnerability keeps you afraid of blending with the wilderness through spiritual connection and bound to the material support offered by your uncivilization, which keeps you servile and submitted.

"Our knowledge is what your people have forgotten about your true origins, nature, purpose, and destiny. This is why the lower powers that have taken over the Earth are trying desperately to deny and cover up our existence, turning it into ridicule for the public to keep ignoring the message we carry, while secretly waging a covert genocide against my people.

"It all started in the times when the civilization you known as Atlantis, emerged as a new seat of powers for the Star Council on Earth, and continents were divided between factions. Old Lemuria, our motherland where my people and much later yours were first conceived and born, had developed into a planetary civilization with a network of colonies and outposts around the world, many of which have left remains that still can be seen today. After ages of Peace and Consciousness, the divisions in the heavens reached our planet, and the star Council established here could keep it safe and united.

"Nevertheless, after some time, a faction of star people based in Atlantis fell into the temptation of power and greed and went away from the greater Divine Law and Cosmic Order, that they were originally meant to maintain and protect on our young Earth. After winning battles over our Earth and succeeding in pushing back invading forces, they claimed ownership and dominion over our home planet, which is not their home, and to which they were sent to keep watch and protect. Their claim was denied by the Council of Star Elders keeping the Cosmic Order, so the faction of lower principalities rebelled and banded with the invading forces they had been fighting against. They broke the covenant of the planetary watchers by manipulating g genetics and breeding several experimental races of hybrids and slave species for their own interest and power.

"As opposed to the creation of my people and yours that was approved by the higher Council of Star Elders within a cosmic plan for soul consciousness and planetary evolution, these genetic manipulations were done for selfish purposes by the lower principalities against the higher Divine Law and Cosmic Order. Those artificially produced species, including giants, dragons, and monsters, (mythical creatures) were used as slaves and soldiers in wars against the Star Council of Elders, still based at Mu. Your most ancient cultures have kept the memories of those wars involving star fleets in their sacred archives and ancestral legends that have survived to this day.

"My people and your people took part side by side in those star wars to maintain the Divine Law and reestablish the Cosmic Order of the Star Council on this Mother Earth, our home planet. My people stood all the time with the Council of Star Elders based in Lemuria, our Motherland. But your people got divided, many falling under the influence of the lower lords, based in Atlantis. Some of them were enslaved in their army and we had to fight them. As time passed, the conquering powers of the lower lords devised new ways to transform again the genetics of your people, turning them more into easily servile creatures with less spiritual consciousness and psychic abilities to take over the whole world."

As you can clearly read that humans are repeating the story of Atlantis in this current time and as most of us know, Atlantis was destroyed, some say by their lust for power, their lack of spirituality and respect for life.

Elder Kamooch continued his story about his species, "As the strongest and most powerful psychic beings on this home-planet, the task of my people was to defend, as our younger brothers, those of your people who had stayed truthful to the Divine Law, even from the ones among yours who posed a threat. For that reason, the fallen powers started waging a war of extermination on my people that has not yet ended to this day, except that it is being done in secret.

"Those events caused the separation of your people from my people. From there came the many accounts depicting us as dangerous cannibals, under which your people unfortunately too often know us. Some of our species have indeed attacked and killed, and even eaten some of yours, and sometimes abducted individuals for attempts of contact, and even interbreeding. But these individual actions cannot be taken out of the context of wars of resistance to the destruction of homelands, just like many of your tribal people have reacted to invasion when their very survival was threatened by enemies.

"But the truth is that many more of my species have been destroyed by Human actions than we have ever hurt your people. Our total population has been reduced to a few thousand last survivors scattered around this home-planet. To this day, most of us still die from Human hands rather than from natural causes. Since this world has become hostile to us, we have chosen to reproduce as little as possible, for safety.

"This modern Humanity, which you call Homo Sapiens, was encoded to be totally depending on external material support, with more rational minds and less spiritual empathy and sensibility, to serve the agenda of taking over all other life forms on this home-planet for the sole interest of the lower lords, who set themselves as powers against the Divine Law. Today, my people represent the last and only species that your species has not yet dominated, but this submission from us will never happen. This is the reason why the lower lords and the powers they control have been trying to eliminate my people.

"When the new Atlantean race conquered the world, the exterminated systematically not all of my people that they could find, but also the largest part of your Lemurian ancestry, except for a few remote tribal populations. As this modified and reprogrammed Humanity invaded all parts of the world, the last survivors of my people, to assure our survival, had to keep moving further away from the threat into the most remote wilderness and places where your species can hardly reach, including the network of deep caves in the underworld, with some of your Lemurian ancestors. But even there, we have been hunted down by the powers of the lower lords; nowhere is left safe. Eventually, ages later, they succeeded in destroying the whole continent of Lemuria, mainly through geothermal explosions.

"So, my people disappeared from your official stories, books, and collective memory. Tribal cultures that have kept living in the wilderness and maintained their spiritual abilities could still see us. But after time, even your tribal peoples slowly lost their psychic powers and their ability to communicate with us, being entrapped with the whole planet in the power grid of the lower lords, except for the seers, who also ended up being rare. So, the communication between my people and yours got almost completely lost in the last few of your generations. We are now known mainly through legends, often depicting the worst parts of our history and behaviors. Most of your people stopped believing in our existence and we are usually met by fear from the ones who learn about us. Because of this separation, we have been forced to stay away from your people and must often play the card of frightening away unwelcome intruders who are not ready to communicate with us, for our own safety and survival.

"The new uncivilization that rules your world had been banned from the Star Council, which left from our home-planet until a later evolutionary leap. Those same powers serving the lower lords are keeping this Earth enslaved today, through a combination of means including control of the information, mind programming, staged events, and a series of advanced technologies like holographic images. They want you to forget how they take over control of your home-planet and destiny through illegitimate means and have kept your people enslaved, making you more and more dependent on new technologies.

"They want you to forget the Divine Law and Cosmic Order that we have protected with our Star Ancestors, with whom we have kept in contact. As proof of their dominion, the lower lords want you to keep destroying our home-planet, which is not their home, and that they have invaded for their own selfish interest and powers. Since they have laid the basis and frames of your known civilization and have set the stage for most major events influencing your collective consciousness and destiny, to push forward their agenda of global control (and universal control), all of your people have fallen under their material and psychic enslavement to some extent and level, none has been left untouched by their detrimental influence.

"My people are seeking those among yours who are willing and able to help us in making Peace again between elder and younger brothers, and in joining again in our long-time common mission to free our home-planet from the grip and grid of the lower lords. Our common goal, which is also our ultimate responsibility and duty, is to realign our planetary Soul and civilization with the Divine Law and Cosmic Order, in order to take again righteously our place within the circle of the Star Council."

"You must first start by finding your connection, through Nature, with the Soul of our Mother Earth, which connects us all as relatives. On this path of conscious evolution, you must recover your spiritual gifts and psychic abilities that were encoded in your DNA through your ancestral Star Seeds. As your genetic memory and your soul memory awaken, you will recognize us as elder relatives and allies, and cease to fear us, deny us the right to exist, chase us like beasts, or consider us as more primitive than your species. You will realize how manipulated and controlled your people have been under the rule of the lower lords, and how what your uncivilization remembers of its history is but the last page rewritten and modified, to make you forget about your true origins, nature, purpose, and destiny, as part of a program to keep your people domesticated like pets and enslaved like livestock, in an agenda for global control and tyranny.

"We wait for some of you to awaken to your spiritual abilities and reach out to connect with us, to help us deliver to your people the message and ancient knowledge we have care-kept through the ages, concerning your origins, purpose, and destiny, before it gets completely obliterated from your collective consciousness. We wait for enough of your people to act in togetherness and succeed in freeing the world from its ages-old bondage and curse, to transform your collective karma and evolve into a planetary civilization based on Peace among species, in alignment with the Divine Law and Cosmic Order, to be rehabilitated in the Star Council with our eldest Elders.

"We wish for some like you to come forward and speak for us to your people, to reawaken their collective memory, because your people are gifted with articulated speech and languages, unlike ours, but most of them have forgotten how to communicate through telepathy. There is nothing to prove about us, but our ancient living knowledge, carrying the same message as the Star Elders, is crucial to your next evolutionary quantum leap into a planetary civilization of Peace within the Divine Law. When you reach that level of consciousness evolution, my people and yours will again be brothers and our Elders of the Star Council will return among us to reestablish the Divine Law of the Cosmic Order.

The Warning to Humans

"Unless your collective consciousness returns to a peaceful spiritual civilization of the Soul, you might become one more on a long list of extinct species that have either destroyed themselves or their planet. Those failed sol evolution experiments and world extinctions happen more often than we can tell you. For these reasons, our Star Elders and my people, your Elder Brother, are concerned about your Soul. Your spiritual evolutionary process, although of shorter existence than ours or theirs, is of the greatest significance for us, as it is for them, having assisted to it since its very beginning, at your conception.

It is also of capital importance for all other life forms on this home planet, whose destiny is closely tied to yours and often depends on its outcome. Inter-species peaceful, spiritual relationships start with the other life forms incarnating consciousness in your very immediate environments on your home planet. They are always present for any of you. Animals, plants, and stones are also conscious sentient beings understanding naturally soul telepathy, the psychic gift with which your seers (and Indigenous people) have kept relating to them.

You can choose to ignore the spiritual awakening happening and so much needed to provide hope for this planet or remain in the old indoctrination, enslaving structures and institutions of the lower lords, and keep destroying life on Earth. Then, all this evolution your people have done would have been in vain. Or you can choose to rise above outdated mentalities and behaviors, and evolve into Peace."

David Paulides on Missing 411

Author and former police officer David Paulides wrote a series of books titled, *Missing 411*. His books consist of documented cases of people and children who have vanished without a trace in national parts and elsewhere in America. Paulides is dedicated to proving the reality of Bigfoot. His books publicized the fact that the U.S. National Park Service does not keep an independent list of people that go missing in their parks, and parks in California have refused to talk to him about their missing cases.

Four hundred and seventy people have vanished in Yosemite Park, California, according to Paulides.

Paulides suspects Park officials know what is going on and want to cover it up. He says, "Often, the victims are children whose bodies are later found in seemingly impossible locations. Sometimes these kids that I write about are found, like a 2 or 3-year-old, are found 10-15 miles from the point they were last seen, or they're found 5,000 feet higher in elevation than where they disappeared," Paulides says. "And as a parent, you'll know, my kid wasn't going to make that distance in this amount of time or climb that elevation this period. So, it doesn't make sense."

Could Bigfoot/Sasquatch be blamed for abducting or killing adults and children missing in parks because humans are encroaching on their territory? It seems like a more logical explanation than any other for finding a small child at the summit of a 5,000-foot mountain.

CHAPTER THIRTEEN

The Seward Mystery

Seward is a small port city in southern Alaska, set on an inlet on the Kenai Peninsula. Seward has a population of 2,700 and is known for its offshoring oil drilling and commercial fishing. It's a gateway to Kenai Fjords National Park, where glaciers flow from the Harding Icefield into coastal fjords. Surrounded by peaks, the fjords are a whale and porpoise habitat, and the town is also a hotspot for UFOs. Seward, Alaska is a small fishing village except for the Black Hawk helicopters that roam the skies all night long.

Bill Sleasman has worked at the Seward fish processing plant as a dock foreman for years and has lived in the fishing town since 1984, but what he witnessed one evening in the 1990s was something so extraordinary that he thinks about all the time. He admits he's never seen Bigfoot, but he says in an interview, "I don't believe we are alone in the universe and that many cultures have been seeing them for years such as

Bigfoot, UFOs, and whatever. I've seen what some call UFOs with my own eyes and I know they are out there."

Bill Sleasman with UFO image inserted

Bill's encounter happened years ago in the 1990s, but it is still etched in his memory forever. He was sitting in his log cabin just before sunset and he heard a military helicopter. He grabbed his binoculars and walked outside to investigate. Looking in his binoculars, he spotted a Black Hawk military helicopter without any markings. As he continued to watch for an extended time, the helicopter continued to hover in the sky.

The Sikorsky UH-60 Black Hawk is a four-blade, twin-engine, medium-lift utility military helicopter with a multi-role versatile range of missions like air assault, medevac, command, and control. In recent years, the helicopter was made available for purchase by US commercial companies and civilians.

If the helicopter's presence was strange enough as he headed back to his cabin, he froze in his steps. "It was like a starship," he claimed. "It was huge!"

Bill estimated the starship was 1,500' to 2,000' feet long, 400' feet to 600' feet wide, 50' feet high, and positioned 350' feet in the air. "It was big, it was beautiful, and a silver-gray color!" It was close enough that Bill could make out the details. "It had a type of crystal right in the middle of it that was emitting brilliant blue, reddish, white lights. This thing dwarfed a super tanker."

As he stared at it, a weird feeling crept over him as if an energy-type power was controlling him. It felt like his body was humming. After several minutes, he went back into his house and called his neighbor, asking if they could see what he was seeing above his home. They said they could see the UFO. He hung up after talking to neighbors and grabbed a chair and returned outside to watch the display and watched the starship for hours. The next thing Bill remembers he was waking up inside his cabin. He can't remember returning to the house and what time he returned. He lost several hours of time, common with alien abductions. But there's one thing he knows for sure that whatever he saw that night was not of this world, and others witnessed it too.

The next morning when he was driving to work, he was listening to KSRM radio with Bob Bird, the morning talk show host. He was receiving hundreds of calls from people who witnessed the same UFO that Bill had seen. People all over the area witnessed the same UFO hovering and casting a light on the water around 12 am to 1 am. At the same time, Bill watched the craft.

Bill Bird said the people calling in to report the UFO witnessed it hover vertically and horizontally and cast a light over Cook Inlet.

Bill Sleasman is convinced the military was involved with the starship and was tracking it. But he understands why the military won't admit UFOs are extraterrestrials—people would never believe it. He theorizes that UFOs like Alaska because of its remote wilderness and there are many places for them to hide.

So, what happened to Bill in the hours erased from his memory? We can only imagine that Bill was taken aboard the craft and examined by the extraterrestrial beings as hundreds of abductees have claimed through the years. If only Bill could have been regressed through hypnosis, we might learn what happened to him during his hours of missing time.

Mysteries abound where most we seek answers. – Ray Bradbury, Science Fiction author

CHAPTER FOURTEEN

Healed by Aliens

MUFON Investigator Preston Dennett has investigated and accumulated hundreds of stories on UFO abductions, sightings, and even healings by extraterrestrials by eyewitnesses and from MUFON archived files and has written 20 books on those cases.

One of the leading factors pointing toward the veracity of UFO healing is the extraordinary number of cases. The fact that most major researchers have uncovered these types of cases is clearly not a coincidence. One of the early researchers, Don Worley, contributed to the following case involving a woman who injured herself aboard a UFO because of fighting against her abductors. Her experience reveals why some ETs, despite the technology to heal people, choose not to heal them with certain conditions.

As Dennett wrote, "Anyone who has done even the smallest amount of objective research into the subject of UFOs knows that UFOs are real." Why are they here or have they been here for eons, observing humans and even genetically experimenting on us? Dennett believes they are neither invaders nor saviors, only here to study us.

In his book, *The Power of UFOs: 300 True Account of People Healed by Extraterrestrials*, he writes about U.S. veteran Ruth Simmons of Alaska who experienced a remarkable UFO healing after being injured aboard a UFO during an abduction. She reported being taken many times and believed one of the reasons she was chosen by the ETs is because "I am very strong." Despite this, the encounters are frightening, and she sometimes tries to resist them.

"I was on a table in an upright or standing position," she says, describing the 2013 encounter in which she was healed, "and around me were four little beige aliens, two tall blonds, and a dark, curly-haired man. They had secured my upper body and were attempting to secure my legs. While they were doing this a robotic arm was moving into position over my lower abdomen. I kicked my left leg up and actually impaled myself on a sharp edge that was under the robotic arm. The little beige aliens became frantic, and I got the feeling that they were distressed, like, 'She hurt herself! She hurt herself.'

What happened next can only be described as incredible. "One of the blond aliens came and put his hand over my injury and wiped off my leg. And then I saw that my leg was healed. But there was a scar! That is when the dark-haired man *mind-talked* to me and told me not to worry, the scar would eventually fade away and my leg would look as if it always had."

Earlier, Simmons had given birth by C-section, and now had an unsightly scar and stretch marks. During her experience, she decided to make a request. "I asked him to get rid of my C-section and my stretch marks."

The man smiled, "I can't do that," he said.

"Why not?" Simmons inquired.

"Because people will know we are here."

"Well, what if I tell people that you are here? Simmons replied.

"Well, no one will believe you."

"Yep," said Simmons. "You are right, no one will."

Axe Wound Healing in Alaska

This story comes from researcher and author Ardy Sixkiller Clarke and involves the healing of an axe-wound on the foot. The witness is also a "medicine woman," working for the health and wellness of her community.

"Some people call me a medicine woman," says Belle, a Native American from Alaska. "But I don't like the title, medicine woman. I'm just an old woman who knows about plants."

Belle lives in a remote Alaskan village with about forty houses. Not far from the village is a sacred field where the "Star People," come and visit with the local population. "They are our ancestors, and they care about us, but some are also scientists. They measure the levels of pollution, they examine the Earth and the plants to determine if there are poisons that are changing them," says Belle.

On one occasion (date not given circa 2000s) Belle was healed by the ETs. "I was chopping wood one day and I hit my foot with the axe. It went all the way through my shoe into my foot. By the time I freed myself from the axe, my shoe was filled with blood. All my kids were at school. I tied a dishrag around my foot and tried to stop the blood. Suddenly, they (the Star People) appeared, and they untied the dishcloth, and with their hands they took away the pain and the bleeding. After that, I walked normal and never had any problems. There is still a scar though...the Star People saved me."

CHAPTER FIFTEEN

Where did They go?

Nome, Alaska sits right on the coast of the Bering Sea and is incredibly isolated and relatively desolate with less than 22 square miles of land and water that make up the city. If a UFO was going to show up, it would be in an area such as this—one of the most unusual places in Alaska with minimal human life. What is surprising is that there are no roads or even a ferry system leading into or out of Nome, so once you're there, you're stuck until the next flight comes along.

Nome is also known for its incredibly harsh winters. Between November and March, it is common to have temps well below zero degrees and ranging between minus 10 and minutes 55 degrees Fahrenheit. The frozen wonderland and dark sky can take its toll on even the most seasoned humans.

My cousin Martin, an engineer, spent a year at McMurdo Research Station in Antarctica inside a domed structure with several researchers. He said the dark days and nights can make a person hallucinate and go a little crazy. At night, his dreams consisted of horrible nightmares.

With a year-round population of under 4,000 residents, the small community of Nome isn't known for being a major economic hub or a place that tourists flock to. In fact, what seems to have gotten the most people talking about this isolated community is the mysterious disappearances of 24 people that happened between the 1960s and 2004. These all occurred in Nome and throughout the surrounding villages.

Initially, the Nome, Alaska disappearances were believed to be the work of a serial killer. The reasoning was that a serial killer had to be involved due to the large number of people that had gone missing. Family and friends of the missing people, as well as the whole community, were on edge 24/7 thinking about who could be lurking around their community and praying for the innocent.

Although you might not expect these large numbers of disappearances to occur in such a remote and desolate area, you might be surprised to learn that there are roughly 350 miles of roads radiating from Nome that led deep into some of Alaska's most scenic, pristine country. The rugged and lonely vastness would be easy to disappear into and never be found. Translation: hundreds of miles of private roads that are perfect for a UFO abduction or worse, dumping a body.

The Nome, Alaska disappearances gained such worldwide attention that Hollywood made a mostly fictionalized movie called *The Fourth Kind* released in 2009, that revolved around alien abductions. The sci-fi thriller was set in the town and largely told the tale of how a whole town disappeared in Alaska—the missing people in Nome, Alaska were assumed to be abducted by a UFO. The movie was later found to be largely misleading as it was marketed as a documentary but in fact, was just a misrepresentation of facts surrounding these disappearances. The movie is a conspiracy theory that centers around the reason for the missing people being abducted by aliens.

What is the truth behind the missing people? Is it a UFO, alien abduction, serial killer, or simply human error? Through FBI investigation, it was determined that these disappearances were largely a combination of excessive alcohol consumption and a harsh winter climate. If you head to the bar and load up on drink too much thinking that you will just walk home afterward, don't bank on making it too far in the frigid temperatures that await you outdoors. Hypothermia can develop in as little as five minutes in temperatures of minus 50 degrees Fahrenheit if you're not dressed properly and have exposed skin, especially the scalp, hands, fingers, and face.

Even if someone died from hypothermia, there is always a body to recover. None were found, which leaves an even greater mystery. Although these tragic events have left a dark stain on the community of Nome, the people are tough and resilient even during the toughest of times.

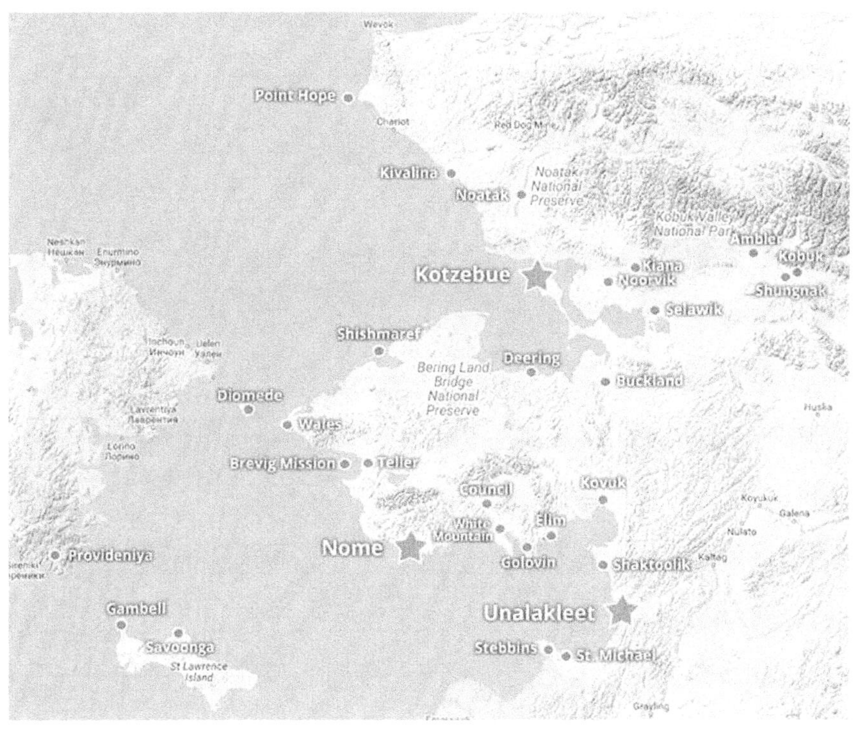

CHAPTER SIXTEEN

Alaska's Hauntings

Alaska was purchased from Russia in 1876 and in 1890 the massive migration of miners and settlers moved to Alaska for the great gold rush. In 1912, Alaska was granted territorial status in 1912 by the United States of America.

Author Jack London caught the Klondike gold fever at the age of twenty-one when he stepped ashore in Alaska in 1897. It was a time that brought thousands of people to the frigid land when America was suffering from acute economic depression.

London spent the winter in the Yukon from 1897 to 1898, gathering vivid experiences which would later become his famous novella, *The Call of the Wild*, published in 1903.

During that time, more than 30,000 people traveled to the area, and people fought and died over their gold claims. Saloons and hotels became haunted.

With majestic snowcapped mountains as a backdrop, Skagway, Alaska has been a port town since 1897 and can be found in the most northern part of southeast Alaska, about one hundred miles north of Juneau. Skagway today is still the farthest northern port along the inside passage.

The town became famous because of its location as a shipping port, and it was a convenient spot to drop off people from Seattle on their way to the Klondike in search of gold. The temperatures there even during winter are more temperate than other Alaska towns.

Except for its paved streets, Skagway appears physically today much like it was in 1897 when it sprang up because of the turn-of-the-century Klondike Gold Rush. The town's population in 1897 was 700 residents, which swelled to around 20,000 in 1898. Interestingly, by 1899, the population went back down to 700 people. Because the town never burned down or fell apart, it became part of the Klondike Gold Rush National Historical Park. fly in by plane. Some hearty souls do come up the road from British Columbia to Whitehorse in the Yukon and then travel back down route 2 to Skagway.

The ghosts who haunted Skagway from the wild gold rush period of 1897-'98, when lawlessness was rampant, corruption and evil doings were commonplace, and many people suffered unexpected, unhappy deaths because of the horrible situations that existed here or were allowed to take place. To top it all off, a diphtheria epidemic swept through town killing many children. With people coming to bad, sudden ends, their dreams also were snuffed out. All these situations are ghost-making ones.

The following stories were taken from HauntedHouses.com:

The Red Onion Saloon

The Red Onion Saloon was originally built to be a brothel. The white building, with dark trim, has two stories, with a storefront window. The first floor was then and is now a saloon, and the second floor has ten small rooms called cribs.

In 1898, the ladies of the night working at this establishment serviced their customers there. Now an office, some of the dressing rooms are for employees, and a refurbished bedroom called the Madam's Room occupies the second floor.

Ghostly hauntings on the Second Floor is believed to be caused by at least one female presence, who is sometimes hostile toward men. Footsteps have been heard upstairs when no one living is there. A spooked employee once called the police, who also heard running feet and pounding on the second floor. When the employee complained, arriving officers went to investigate and saw a shadowy figure go down the hall and slip into the Madam's Room. Nothing visible was there.

* Cold patches and areas upstairs have been felt by employees.
* The strong aroma of perfume permeates and travels along the second-floor hall.
* Some unseen presence likes to be helpful, and waters the living plants on the second floor, when no living persons were present to do this chore.
* The shadowy form of a woman has been seen watering non-existing plants in the Madam's Room.
* A musician who once lived on the second floor for a short period, while playing downstairs in the Saloon, woke one night to see a shimmering light in his room that gave him a very cold sensation.
* One of the local town leaders has felt twice in the hall a strong presence, in sort of a hostile mood.

The Golden North Hotel

The Golden North Hotel is a three-story building and sports a corner cupola facing the street. Rooms 14 and 23 are known to have the most manifestations. Room 23 is the favorite haunt of a pretty, young woman entity nick-named Mary by the staff. She died in the hotel from pneumonia, while waiting for her beloved to return from the gold fields, and while trying to hide from the local ruffians as well.

* Mary has fully appeared to various hotel employees, mainly the chambermaids and maintenance men.
* The owner and one of the maids both together saw Mary standing by the window in room 23, looking out of the window.
* A hotel guest singer from Juneau, had his girlfriend take his picture while standing in the then-empty third-floor hall. Imagine his surprise when the picture was developed to see standing right next to him, the detailed apparition of a young woman, known as Mary!
* Other people visiting room 23 have felt the sensation of being choked as if one was suffering from pneumonia.
Room 14 is another favorite haunt of either Mary or another ghost, and perhaps both!
* The full apparition of Mary has been seen in room 14 as well.
* A grayish light form moves around the room at night.
* While staying in the room, some hotel guests felt sick, to the point of almost passing out. Then, a grayish light form appears to them and gradually fades away. The guests then suddenly don't feel sick anymore.
* Four ghost hunters spent the night in Room 14. The next morning, they found a ring around the tub, that wasn't there the night before, as if some unseen entity took a bath. They had not used the tub.

Eagles Hall

The second floor seems to be the favorite spot for several friendly ghosts, who make their presence known by moving cold spots. People have felt the presence of these unseen entities, keeping them company on the second floor.

Haunted Victorian House

The "graceful, Victorian residence" was built in 1904, and was the home of the Mulvihill family from 1914 to 1949. William "Mul" Mulvihill was the chief dispatcher for the White Pass and Yukon Railroad and kept a telegraph key in his house.

Manifestations have been reported by past owners—the entity is believed to be William Mulvihill.

* Doors throughout the house open and close by themselves.

* An unseen entity likes to walk up and down the stairs with heavy footsteps.

* The sound of a telegraph key can be heard clicking away.

The White House

Originally built as a private home, the White House became a hospital during World War II, then a small hotel, a day-care center, and finally a home to various families. It was abandoned in 1988 after it was damaged by fire but has been restored to its former glory. It is now a haunted upscale bed and breakfast.

* A commercial fisherman and his family were staying there. He and his wife awoke one night to see the detailed apparition of a woman, standing at the foot of their bed.

* The couple's three-year-old daughter happily chatted away with an apparition in the kitchen, who matched the description of the woman they saw in their bedroom. This gentle woman specter is believed to be the woman who used to run a daycare in this house.

Whitter, Alaska Mystery

Alaska is a large and mostly unoccupied state. There are many ghost towns and abandoned villages all over the place. And this abandoned Alaska military building in Whittier could be arguably one of the most haunted places in Alaska. After decades of neglect, this old building has completely fallen into ruin.

There's a tiny town called Whittier, located on the Prince William Sound in Alaska. This little spot is the site of one of the most haunted buildings in Alaska. The Buckner Building was commissioned during World War II and completed in 1953.

General Simon Buckner commissioned the bunker to be built to protect American troops during the war. The Buckner Building was built to be six stories tall, and about 500 feet long by 50–150 feet wide. The entire structure is approximately 275,000 square feet, and once housed a giant mess hall, large sleeping quarters, a movie theatre, a bowling alley, a small jail, and even tunnels connecting the town of Whittier, Alaska.

On March 27, 1964, the building felt the 9.2 megathrust earthquake but suffered almost no damage. Across south-central Alaska the ground opened up collapsing structures, and a tsunami was generated from the earthquake that caused about 131 deaths.

The military pulled out in 1966 and abandoned the building, where it went through several hands before passing to the City of Whittier. The building fell into disrepair.

Everything inside the building and out has been broken and vandalized. While people are no longer allowed inside, but through the year the building was destroyed by disrespectful visitors, and underwent a constant freeze-thaw cycle, as the windows and doors were all removed and damaged.

Numerous reports include strange sounds emanating from deep within the building. Nature has slowly begun to reclaim the building after it was abandoned, and many animals live inside. There have also been strange sightings in and around the building.

Juneau's Historic Alaskan Hotel

Juneau's historic Alaskan Hotel has a haunted history. One sailor decided to seek out the ghosts, but it didn't end well. Bettye Adams owned the Alaskan Hotel for more than 40 years. "I just – it's creepy. You know, I've never seen anything, but I feel things," she said.

Room 315 has two spartan-looking single beds with floral linen. There's a painting of two women from the early century. I can't be sure, but they appear to be working girls. And a replica antique phone hangs on the wall. There aren't many clues that you're still in the 21st century. Now that we're standing in Room 315, Adams claims this room isn't unique.

"I would think there's just as much haunting on the second floor," Adams said. "There's all kinds of haunting in the bar, in the basement, all kinds of things."

Adams proceeded to tell a disturbing story about Room 315. "It was May 19, 2007. A guided missile cruiser, the USS Bunker Hill was in port but was due to leave the next day. And one of the sailors on it just emailed us and said he wanted the 'haunted room' and we were like 'whatever... and put him here," Adams said.

Juneau police officer Chris Gifford recalls getting a call about a disturbance at the Alaskan. There was a Navy ship in. There were a lot of people downtown that probably hadn't been off the boat for a long time," Gifford said.

Gifford switched on his recorder as he and his partner arrived at the hotel at about a quarter to twelve. "So, we went there, there's a band playing," Gifford said. "I remember a band playing in the bar and people kind of just directing us to the upstairs."

The door to Room 315 was locked. "We're still knocking on the door and a guy comes up and kind of whispers to me, 'Hey I think your guy just jumped out the window,'" Gifford said.

22-year-old Americorps volunteer Jill Weitz was staying in a room below and said, "I remember hearing yelling but kind of just assumed that it was coming from the bar downstairs. We hear glass shatter from above and within moments our window within our hotel room just shatters."

The next building is only a few feet away. Caught between the buildings, the sailor apparently broke more than one window on his way down. "His body hitting the window and shattering the glass into our rooms and then proceeded to fall downward and was mind-bending, to say the least," Weitz said.

The police officers broke down the door. "The walls were covered in blood," Gifford said. "There was—it looked like something very bad had happened in there and I didn't know what it was but it didn't look normal."

Gifford said they didn't know what to think except that someone was badly hurt down below. "You know, under Juneau you can see that it's really built on pilings, the city really is," Gifford said. "It's like a tunnel down there and I didn't know how to get into that tunnel if I needed to—we were going to have to figure that out."

Incredibly, the young sailor was able to walk and made it to the street. "He had injuries all over his body from head to toe," Gifford said.

The man was medevaced out of Juneau and survived his injuries. Bettye Adams said Navy Officcrs arrived the next morning to investigate. It was understood that they didn't want publicity. There wasn't anything in the newspaper. But... "His mother called me from Arizona and said, 'What do you mean renting a room that is haunted? You nearly killed my son,'" Adams said. "And I said, 'I really-really have nothing to do with that.'"

Adams said guests rarely report ghostly encounters, though..."It's with employees that it's a real problem and they quit and go away," Adams said. "But not everyone who works there. "I've never been spooked or seen nothing, or I found people who weren't supposed to be here but they were in the flesh,' local musician Scott Fry said. Fry has worked at the hotel since the '90s. "There was a guy here last winter who swore that there was a whole SWAT team out back on the hillside ready to come in and get him but I think that might've been induced some other way."

There has been a lot written about the Alaskan Hotel. Juneau writer Bjorn Dihle wrote the book, *Haunted Inside Passage,* which gives a version of this incident. "You know when you think about it, history is a ghost story. And the more you think about history the haunting it becomes," Dihle said. "But I know that if you think hard enough about something, especially if you're confined in a dirty little room, thinking about it, after having a few drinks, you might think you see something. Our minds are so fickled and weak and vast at the same time."

This horror story could have ended tragically. But is it a ghost story? The only one who might have an answer is a Navy veteran who at his own request was put in a so-called haunted room at the Alaskan Hotel.

The Ghosts of Sitka, Alaska

Sitka's history began as the ice that covered much of Southeast Alaska began to recede. According to a Tlingit legend, Mount Edgecumbe, a 3,200-foot-tall dormant volcano, located on southern Kruzof Island, was the smoking beacon that brought the original native Tlingit Indians to Sitka around 10,000 years ago.

Sitka was originally inhabited by a major tribe of Tlingits, who called the village "Shee Atika." It was discovered by the Russian Vitus Bering expedition in 1741, and the site became "New Archangel" in 1799. St. Michael's Redoubt trading post and fort were built here by Alexander Baranof, manager of the Russian-American company. Tlingits burned down the fort and looted the warehouse in 1802. In 1804, the Russians retaliated by destroying the Tlingit Fort, in the Battle of Sitka. This was the last major stand by the Tlingits against the Russians, and the Indians evacuated the area until about 1822. By 1808, Sitka was the capital of Russian Alaska. Baranof was Governor from 1790 through 1818.

During the mid-1800s, Sitka was the major port on the North Pacific coast, with ships calling from many nations. Furs destined for European and Asian markets were the main export, but salmon, lumber, and ice were also exported to Hawaii, Mexico, and California. After the purchase of Alaska by the U.S. in 1867, it remained the capital of the Territory until 1906, when the seat of government was moved to Juneau.

A Presbyterian missionary, Sheldon Jackson, started a school, and in 1878 one of the first canneries in Alaska was built in Sitka. During the early 1900s, gold mines contributed to its growth. During World War II, the town was fortified, and the U.S. Navy built an air base on Japonski Island across the harbor, with 30,000 military personnel and over 7,000 civilians. After the war, the BIA converted some of the buildings to be used as a boarding school for Alaska Natives,

Mt. Edgecumbe High School. The U.S. Coast Guard now maintains the air station and other facilities on the Island. A large pulp mill began operations at Silver Bay in 1960 and closed in 1993.

The ghosts of Sitka haunt Sitka's beautiful terrain. From its turbulent history of battles, hangings, prostitution, and opium dens to disappearing ships.

The old Russian buildings hold the spirits of young children who died tragically in the harsh new land of the 1800s and have been seen playing in the buildings.

Haunted Tanana Valley Fairground

Who would ever think that a fun place like a fairground would be haunted, but Tanana Valley State Fairgrounds north of Fairbanks, Alaska is extremely haunted.

The Fairgrounds was constructed in 1924 and each year in August it comes alive with people and children, except for one building that is the home to a dark entity. Lloyd Husky, the fairground's manager has witnessed its power. One night while he was working late at Badger Hall in his office, he felt and presence, and suddenly a book flew off his bookshelf, and then a chair rolled across the room by itself. He left the office quickly.

Doreen Low, a security guard at the fairgrounds, was physically attacked while shutting off the water at Badger Hall. She said it felt like something smack her on the back of the head with force, and at first, thought it was a co-worker in the other room. She looked down at the floor to see a sanding sponge. Next, they went to one of the restrooms and hand soap began pouring out of the dispenser, and paper towels were flying out of the holder.

Doreen and her co-worker fled the bathroom.

A newspaper reporter named Darrell decided to investigate the Fairground's history and discovered one hundred years earlier a brutal attack by a Fairgrounds worker on a child had occurred there. Darrel spent the night in the building and said he was spooked by the cold energy that permeated the building. His magnetometer began spiking and he heard footsteps walking throughout the room. At times muffled voices could be heard.

Theories suggest that this is not a haunting but poltergeist activity from a tragedy that happened in the past and that energy manifests itself in the building where the attack occurred. Theories suggest that glass with its crystalline structure holds onto residual energy and EVPs (electronic voice phenomenon). That energy is pressed inside the glass and is replayed from time to time like a broken tape recorder. Such an event leaves a scar on the fabric of time.

What are Ghosts?

Because Alaska has a rich history, legends of ghosts and haunted buildings continue. Many hauntings are memory apparition or an intelligent entity who was murdered or died tragically and can't get beyond the tragic experience on the ethereal side. Their energy still lingers.

A placed memory apparition is much easier to comprehend because it is essentially a tape recording of an incident caught in a time loop. The apparition has no consciousness and repeats its fate with cognitive patterns. Although it can be unnerving and often frightening to experience a place memory apparition, there aren't any dilemmas attached to the loop.

Intelligent ghosts and apparitions are scarier because they display thoughts and emotional traits established while alive. If a person was angry and dark, they will remain dark and unfriendly in the spirit world. They are trapped in a limbo existence from their own anger and refusal to move on and evolve.

A ghost is an intelligent entity that interacts with the living, either positively or negatively. Some have accumulated great energy to move objects in a room, and some have been known to harm humans. There are also the stories of children who had untimely deaths, who are trapped in the limbo world and can't understand where they are. That is sad and tragic for the souls of these children.

Some signs of an intelligent haunting are slamming doors or windows, moving objects, i.e., chairs, breaking glasses, turning on the water, causing lights to flicker on and off, and sometimes disembodied voices are heard, such as whispering a name or your name, a cold wind or chill in the room and the strong sense of a presence. Sometimes a full apparition is seen or a dark figure moving in halls or a room.

Poltergeists

Remember the 1982 supernatural horror movie, *Poltergeist*, where a family is besieged by frightening activity and later discover their homes sits on a graveyard.

At first poltergeist activity was theorized to be a mischievous ghost causing the disturbance in a home, but now researchers believe the phenomenon is caused by a "human agent" or someone living in the environment that has strong psychokinesis and a reservoir of unexpressed emotions or sexual tension. If a teen is living in the home, they are usually suspected of powerful telekinetic activity.

The person causing the disturbances usually targets one person due to unresolved issues.

However, most cases of poltergeist activity are short-lived, lasting only days or a few weeks. They rarely stretch out for months or more. Most of the time, they just fade away on their own. So, it is doubtful that Tanana Fairgrounds has a poltergeist, but instead, the fairground is haunted by a dark entity that can't move beyond its limbo existence and attacks humans to express his anger and frustration.

CHAPTER SEVENTEEN

Ghost Ships of Alaska

Kaushik Patowary writes in his 2020 article in *Amusing Planet* that ships aren't meant to sink, but sometimes you have to wonder what miraculous forces kept a vessel afloat. The *SS Baychimo* was such a ship. For nearly four decades after it was abandoned, this 1,300-ton cargo ship sailed the Arctic without fuel or crew, until it disappeared just over fifty years ago, but some believe she is still out there drifting among the frozen icebergs.

Ångermanelfven was used as a trading vessel by her German owners around the Baltic Sea, sailing between Hamburg and Sweden until the First World War began. Following the Great War, she was ceded to the British government as part of Germany's war reparations and was acquired by the Hudson's Bay Company in 1921, whereupon she was renamed *Baychimo*. Based in Ardrossan, Scotland, *Baychimo* made routine trips across the North

Atlantic between her homeport and Canada visiting trading posts and collecting pelts.

In 1923, *Baychimo* was assigned to a different route, this time in the Western Arctic, traveling between Vancouver and the Hudson's Bay Company's posts along the Yukon and Northwest Territories' northern coast. Aside from carrying cargo, *Baychimo* occasionally took passengers, but since she wasn't legally allowed to carry people, these ocean travelers were listed as part of the crew and were required to work on the ship in exchange for a room and a trip back home.

In late September 1931, on her way back to Vancouver, the *Baychimo* ran into a surprise blizzard near Point Barrow on Alaska's northern coast, where she became trapped in pack ice. It became apparent that the crew will have to overwinter in the Arctic, but since *Baychimo* couldn't be heated all winter long, the crew decided to leave the ship and set up camp near the town of Barrow, just over half a mile away. Throughout October and most of November, some men would return to the ship every day to clear away ice from the ship's rudder and other critical pieces of equipment.

On November 24th a powerful blizzard struck, and when it cleared, the men found the *Baychimo* gone. The captain and crew assumed the vessel had sunk, but they soon received word that an Inuk hunter had spotted *Baychimo* roughly 72 km south of their encampment. The crewmen tracked the ship down, but deciding she was unlikely to survive the winter, they removed the most valuable furs from the hold and abandoned the ship for the last time. Captain Cornwell and the remaining crew flew back to Vancouver and the company wrote off the vessel and the negligible cargo it held as a loss.

Shortly thereafter, *Baychimo* was spotted about 480 km to the east of where she was last spotted.

The following year, she was seen again floating near the shores of Alaska. In the decades that followed, numerous people sighted *Baychimo* all around the Arctic peacefully adrift in the frigid waters. Many times, she was boarded by explorers or crews of passing ships, but each time she eluded capture. Once, a group of Alaska Natives boarded her and were trapped aboard for 10 days by a freak storm. In 1969, 38 years after she was abandoned, she was found trapped in an ice pack in the Beaufort Sea between Point Barrow and Icy Cape, off the northwestern Alaskan coast. That was the last recorded sighting of *Baychimo*.

Nearly four decades later in 2006, the Alaskan government began work on a project to find *Baychimo* as well as an estimated 4,000 ships that had disappeared along the coast of Alaska. The search yielded nothing just like the 16,000 people who have vanished in *Alaska's Deadly Triangle*.

Assuming that the *Baychimo* had sunk shortly after her last sighting, it still makes her one of the longest-sailing ghost ships in the world. Ships rarely survive for so long unmanned, especially among the crushing ice packs. It's more than likely that the once unsinkable ghost ship now lies somewhere in the cold, muddy bottom of the Arctic Ocean.

S.S. Baychimo in ice.

CHAPTER EIGHTEEN

Other Bizarre Triangles

Much like the infamous Bermuda Triangle off the coast of Florida, Japan has its deadly triangle known as the Devil's Sea or Devil's Triangle, or the Dragon's Triangle. This mysterious area off the island of Japan has legends of missing vessels and ghost ships drifting without their crew. Located off Japan's coast in the Pacific Ocean and near the Islands of Bonin and a major portion of the Philippine Sea, the Devil's Sea is also known as one of the Vile Vortices found around the planet. These are areas where the pull of the planet's electromagnetic waves is stronger than other parts of the Earth.

Here the ocean depth plunges from 5,748 feet to a maximum depth of 12,276 feet, a convenient place for aliens to have an undersea base, hidden from humans.

Miyake-Jima, a volcanic island off the coast of Japan, is

known for UFO sightings around the volcano, both entering and exiting. In July of 2000, NHK, Japan's State Broadcaster, filmed unknown objects on three occasions during July 2000 on Miyake-Jima Island during volcanic activity.

It is unknown how far the Devil's Sea extends. Interestingly, the Atlantic's Bermuda Triangle has many similarities to the paranormal phenomena taking place in Japan's Devil Triangle where ships, crew, and airplanes vanish without a trace.

The great conqueror Kublai Khan, the fifth Great Khan of the Mongol Empire and the grandson of Genghis Khan, had tried to invade Japan in 1274 and 1281 AD, but both attempts failed after he lost his ships and 40,000 crew members in the Devil's Triangle. Most believe it was due to typhoons or other weather.

In August of 1945, a Mitsubishi A6M Zero supposedly disappeared. A distress radio transmission from the Zero F Wing Commander pilot Shiro Kawamoto crossing the Triangle at the end of the war became an unsolved case. The last thing he said was, "...something is happening in the sky...the sky is opening up."

Because of other ships lost in recent years, the Yokohama Coast Guard Office classified the area as a special danger. The Yomiuri Shimbun newspaper showed a map of the sea with points of several other ships that had vanished in recent years and stated that those ships were lost in the area the Coast Guard had listed as dangerous.

Another story appeared in the *New York Times* about nine ships that vanished in perfect weather in "The Devil's Sea."

Japan's newspaper Yomiuri Shimbun said the area consisted of the Izu Islands and east of the Ogasawara islands, about 200 miles east to west, and about 300 miles north to south, where nine ships were lost in the past five years. Two of the nine ships were lost near Miyake-Jima and Iwo Jima, about 750 miles apart.

In Charles Berlitz's 1989 book, *The Dragon's Triangle*, he theorized that five Japanese military vessels disappeared while on maneuvers near Japanese shores in early 1942. Also, nine modern ships and several hundred crews vanished between 1950 and 1954.

In Daniel Cohen's 1974 book, *Curses, Hexes & Spells,* there are reported legends of the Dragon's Triangle that go back centuries. The use of the name Dragon originated from Chinese fables about dragons existing below the water surface. The fables describe how dragons under the sea attack vessels passing by to satisfy their hunger. Some of the stories originated before the AD period—1000 BC era.

In January 2012, the Chinese freighter MV Lin-je with 19 crew members on board, failed to arrive at the Japanese port of Kagoshima. There was no distress alarm or any signs of problems before the freighter vanished. Even though authorities spent months searching for MV Lin-je, there was no sign of the vessel.

However, Junichi Yaoi, Professor of Ufology at IOND University in Japan, believes there are logical explanations for the disappearances, but not all. Yaoi, author, and expert in paranormal activity claimed the ship was pulled into another dimension during an interview on the 2003 Amazon Prime documentary, "The Devil's Sea."

Professor Yaoi said it was like a radio wave. "TV programs are made in a studio, but when they are broadcast, they are changed into radio waves. So, what I'm saying is, maybe the different dimension is here where we live, but we just can't see or touch it."

The Professor also believes a black hole could be blamed for the disappearances. "Basically, I think some of the tankers sank because of the conditions of the sea during storms." Then he added, "But then they just disappear. I think they go to another dimension...I think an entrance opens in that area."

British biologist and writer Ivan T. Sanderson suggested that hot and cold sea currents crossing the Vile Vortice, lead to the disappearances of ships in the Triangle. According to him, these currents result in electromagnetic disturbances that trap the ships passing by.

Other explanations consist of methane hydrates present on the bottom of the ocean that will explode when it rises about 18° C (64° F). Methane hydrate gases are described as icelike deposits that break off from the bottom and rise, forming bubbles on the surface of the water. The theory goes that these gas eruptions can interrupt buoyancy and can easily sink a ship, leaving no trace of debris.

Another explanation could be the undersea volcanoes around Japan erupt under a vessel and suck it and its crews to the ocean's depths.

Bermuda Triangle

The Bermuda Triangle is another mysterious place where planes, ships and people have vanished. The Bermuda Triangle covers the Straits of Florida, the Bahamas, and the entire Caribbean Island area, the Atlantic east to the Azores. During Christopher Columbus' voyages, he wrote in his logbook about bizarre compass bearings in the area. Luckily, Christopher Columbus didn't disappear.

The Triangle got its name when Vincent Gaddis coined the term 'Bermuda Triangle' in an article for Argosy magazine on the disappearance of Flight 19 where five Avenger Torpedo Bombers disappeared over the Bermuda Triangle on December 5, 1945, after losing contact during a United States overwater navigation training flight from the Naval Air States at Fort Lauderdale, Florida.

A few scientists and researchers believe that time can warp and be warped based on a location. The Triangle is such a location on Earth where the fabric of time is thin and allows travelers to slip through it and emerge in another time or dimension.

The time warp theory came to fruition on December 4, 1970, when Florida pilot Bruce Gernon Jr., his father, and friend Chuck Lafayette were flying toward Bimini Island in the Bahamas in his single-engine aircraft known as Beechcraft Bonanza.

Bruce had made many trips from the Bahamas to Florida and back again, without incident. But December 4 was different. The journey from the Bahamas to Florida usually took one and a half hours, but this trip was made in only 45 minutes.

As Bruce's plane began to gain altitude and reached 10,000 feet, he noticed a dark cloud ahead. As the plane drew closer to the cloud, it grew gigantic every minute. Bruce had no choice but to enter the strange cloud. At first, he managed to go through it and get out of it. But this was not the end. Then he saw another cloud forming in from of him. Inside the second cloud, everything was pitch black, not any light from the sun passed through this cloud.

In Bruce's book, *Beyond the Bermuda Triangle*, he wrote: "Upon entering the cloud, we witnessed an uncanny spectacle. It was dark and black, without rain, and visibility was about four or five miles. There were no lightning bolts, only extraordinarily bright white flashes that would illuminate the entire surrounding area. The deeper we penetrated, the more intense the flashes became, so we made a 135-degree turn to the left and headed due south out of the cloud.

"The remarkable thing is that we did not come out of the

storm 90 miles away from Miami as we should have. We traveled through 100 miles of space in 30 minutes in a little more than three minutes."

The weather that day had been normal, and no rain or thunderstorms were in the forecast. Naturally, Bruce was confused about the black clouds he had entered—one after another. Finally, he saw light ahead, but not light from the sun. Bruce kept flying but the cloud never seemed to end until he was headed toward the sliver of light.

Bruce had a feeling of relief that he was exiting the cloud, but it was short-lived as the exit hole grew shorter, and the entire electronic instruments inside the aircraft stopped functioning. He no longer had control of the single-engine aircraft. It felt as if some unseen force guided his plane.

Finally, he flew out of the tunnel, feeling weightless for a few seconds. He immediately wanted to know his location and contacted ground control about his radar location. He had reached Miami, Florida, but that was impossible. His plane had a speed of 180 km per hour, and they made a trip in 45 minutes. Bruce and his passengers arrived safely in Miami, but others haven't been as fortunate to escape the Triangle's vortex that area ufologists believe can account for UFOs disappearing and reappearing in the sky and how they travel great distances within minutes.

Theories suggest that Bruce's encounter was due to solar sunspots, but there is no record of any huge solar event in 1970. It is theorized that solar wind of 706 km/sec could create a disturbance of the magnetosphere and energy flux transfer. This occurs when a magnetic portal opens in the Earth's magnetosphere through which high energy particles flow from the sun directly into the atmosphere and this caused his compass to spin like a top. They claim this can explain the warping of time.

Lastly, there is the dimensional portal or wormhole theory.

Aliens in the Bermuda Triangle

The existence of a vortex or dimensional gateway created by unknown beings has been speculated by some theorists.

Ufologists suggest that the Triangle is a 'Star Gate' used by extraterrestrials for intergalactic travel.

Many want to believe that Flight 19's disappearance on December 5, 1945, was caused by this UFO stargate. As the planes took off, the weather was clear that day. Lt. Charles Carroll Taylor was supervising the exercise. Five General Motors Eastern Aircraft Division TBM Avenger Torpedo Bombers were never seen again on that day. Fourteen airmen on the flight were lost as well as 13 crew members of a Martin PBM Mariner Flying Boat that launched from Naval Air Station Banana River to search for Flight 19.

Radio conversations went on between the pilots and the base and other aircraft in the area. In a bombing operation, one of the pilots requested and was permitted to drop his last bomb. Forty minutes later, another flight instructor, Lieutenant Robert F. Cox in his FT-74, while forming up with his group of students for the same mission, received an unidentified transmission.

One of the students said, "I don't know where we are. We must have gotten lost after that last turn." Cox then transmitted, "This is FT-74, plane or boat calling 'Powers,' please identify yourself so someone can help you."

Taylor was a seasoned pilot who had made his scheduled pass over hens and chicken shoals in the Bahamas less than an hour earlier but now believed his planes had somehow drifted hundreds of miles off course and ended up in the Florida Keys. Some speculate that the 27-year-old had confused some of the islands of the Bahamas for the Keys.

However, under normal circumstances, pilots lost in the Atlantic were told to point their planes toward the setting sun and fly west toward the mainland. Taylor believed he might be in the Gulf of Mexico. He made the disastrous mistake to steer Flight 19 northeast—a course that would have only taken them even further out to sea. One pilot seemed to recognize that he made a mistake and radioed, "Dammit, if we would just fly west, we would get home."

Taylor finally changed his course and headed west but seemed to change his mind after 6 p.m. when he canceled the order and changed direction. "We didn't go far enough East," he said.

No one knows for sure, but the other pilots probably argued against his decision. Their radio transmissions became faint as their fuel began to run low.

This was Taylor's last radio message, "All planes close uptight. We'll have to ditch unless landfall...when the first plane drops below ten gallons, we all go down together." After that transmission, the only thing heard was an eerie buzz of static.

Several logical theories suggest that the Avengers flew off course and ran out of gas, all crashing into the ocean. Through the years boats have scanned several areas with sonar and have never found any of the planes.

The next morning, the Navy dispatched more than 300 boats and aircraft to search for the missing Flight 19 and the missing search plane Mariner. The search party spent five days combing through more than 300,000 square miles of ocean, but nothing was found. Navy Lieutenant David White made this comment, "We had hundreds of planes out looking, and we searched overland and water for days, and nobody ever found the bodies or any debris."

Some searches continued years later, but no underwater wreckage of the doomed flight was even found even with the most sophisticated sonar and radar equipment.

In 1991, treasure hunter Graham Hawkes announced that he had found the wreckage of the five Avengers off the coast of Florida, but that tail numbers revealed they didn't belong to Flight 19. In 2004, a BBC Documentary showed Hawkes using a new submersible in the same area and identifying one of the planes by its bureau number 23990 as a flight that had crashed on October 9, 1943, over two years before Flight 19. That crew survived.

Ocean Methane Gas Theory

Another theory suggests there are pockets of methane gas, known as methane gas hydrates, that can erupt from the ocean floor and can cause an underwater landslide or seismic wave. But this theory doesn't hold water either.

Another theory suggests that methane is released from time to time from the ocean floor that causes a ship to lose its buoyance and sink. Or the methane floats skyward and causes a plane to stall or even ignite the engine. But that sounds ludicrous.

Although the United States Geological Survey has determined underwater hydrates exist worldwide, no known gas hydrates have occurred in the Bermuda Triangle for the past 15,000 years. Other theories for the Triangle's disappearances include pirates, large waves, wormholes, the Atlantean crystal, and government testing.

Atlantis and Edgar Cayce

Some authors and researchers believe that the continent of Atlantis sank into the ocean eons ago and much of it lies in the Atlantic Ocean. The American clairvoyant Edgar Cayce (1877-1945) gave thousands of readings in a trance-like state on healing, Egypt, and Atlantis. Those readings were documented between 1924-1944 about the lost city of Atlantis and the Atlantean people who achieved the most technologically advanced culture in the world. Their technology includes DNA and genetic experiments, flying and underwater craft, the "Firestone," a gigantic crystal used for power, and temples of healing before a series of catastrophic events destroyed the continent circa 10,000 B.C.

According to Cayce, Atlantis extended from the Gulf of Mexico to Gibraltar. He said that the Bahamas Banks were the last part of Atlantis to sink. In one of his transcendental states, he mentioned an island, Bimini, that had energy crystals used to fuel the city. There was also one giant crystal, the firestone, used to power their flying craft and even destroy cities.

Some believe that Cayce's description of the firestone beneath the ocean activates during certain planetary conditions in the Bermuda Triangle. The mighty crystal creates electromagnetic forces and causes airplanes' and ships' electronic systems to malfunction. That energy is so intense that it propels them into a dimensional vortex.

The Mary Celeste Ship Mystery

The British brig Dei Gratia was about 400 miles east of the Azores on December 5, 1872, when the crew members spotted a ship adrift in the turbulent seas. Captain David Morehouse was shocked to find that the unguided vessel was the Mary Celeste, which had left New York City eight days before him and should have already arrived in Genoa, Italy.

Morchouse changed course to offer help. He sent a boarding party to the ship. Below decks, the ship's charts had been tossed about, and the crewmen's belongings were still in their quarters. The ship's only lifeboat was missing, and one of its two pumps had been disassembled. Three and a half feet of water was sloshing in the ship's bottom through the cargo of 1,701 barrels of industrial alcohol was largely intact. There was still a six-month supply of food and water, which ruled out piracy.

This became one of the most durable mysteries in nautical history. What happened to the ten people who had been aboard the Mary Celeste? Many theories were considered from a mutiny to pirates at sea, sea monsters, and killer waterspouts. In Arthur Conan Doyle's 1884 short story based on the case, he suggested a vengeful ex-slave killed the crew. But there were never any bodies found that would indicate a struggle.

In the 2007 documentary, *The True Story of the Mary Celeste,* investigators offered no definite conclusions but suggested that a faulty chronometer, rough seas, and a clogged pump, could have led Briggs to order the crews to abandon it after sighting land on November 25, 1872.

According to the last entry in the ship's logbook on that fateful day, the Mary Celeste was within sight of the Azores Island of Santa Maria, some 500 miles from where the Dei Gratia would find it nine days later. If there were survivors, why weren't they ever reported?

Mary Celeste photograph taken in Nova Scotia.

Michigan's Triangle

Lake Michigan, in the United States, has been the site of countless sightings of strange objects and phantom planes.

According to marine historian Dwight Bower in his book "Strange Adventures of the Great Lakes" the Michigan Triangle legend was born in 1937, when Captain George Donner unaccountably vanished from his freighter cabin during a routine coal delivery.

Having given strict instructions to be woken from his bed as the ship drew into port, Donner was nowhere to be found three hours later—despite his cabin door being locked from the inside.

Thirteen years later, Northwest Airlines Flight 2501 carrying 55 passengers and three crew left New York City for Minneapolis, only to seemingly evaporate from thin air as it passed over the Michigan Triangle. The wreckage has never been discovered, despite being the subject of an annual search by the Michigan Shipwreck Research Associates, and investigations still continue in trying to explain the incident.

CHAPTER NINETEEN

Evidence of a Portal

Skinwalker Ranch, just 30 miles west of Vernal in northeastern Utah, is one of the most infamous places in the world for paranormal and UFO activity. According to the Ute Indians of northeast Utah, a portal exists in the sky that allows aliens to come and go instantly in the Universe.

Since real estate mogul Brandon Fugal purchased the Skinwalker Ranch from billionaire businessman Robert Bigelow in 2016, a team of researchers and scientists have been conducting experiments at the Ranch to understand the fluctuations of radiation in certain areas of the Ranch, why the team picks up strange radio transmission of 1.6 gigahertz whenever they conduct experiments in the triangle area of the Ranch that causes instruments to malfunction and UAPs to appear in the sky. The docuseries, *The Secret of Skinwalker Ranch*, on the History Channel, is now in its fourth season.

During episode 9, filmed in 2022, the team including Dr. Travis Taylor continued to fire rockets into an area of the Ranch deemed "the triangle" where rockets explode or vanish and mysterious UAPs appear in the sky above it.

During the episode, the group of Ranch investigators and Dr. Taylor invited scientists from Lunasonde to the Ranch to conduct low-frequency radio waves experiments with a special balloon that was released with equipment 70,000 feet above the triangle area. Lunasonde makes the underground world visible, fundamentally transforming our understanding of the planet we live on through their revolutionary low-frequency radar.

The Ranch has been owned by two ranchers, Bigelow and now Brandon Fugal. Through the years, cattle mutilations have taken place, horses killed, a fiery orb that killed a dog, UFOs hovering over the Ranch, fluctuations in the magnetic field and radiation, a huge black animal that was captured on camcorder attacking a llama at the Ranch, strange lights emanating from the Mesa, and one person claimed to see a UFO fly into the Mesa. Inexplicably instruments and equipment constantly fail. During one of the episodes, Superintendent of Skinwalker Ranch Thomas Winterton received a high dose of radiation that sent him to the hospital. Even Dr. Travis Taylor received ionizing radiation while exploring Homestead 2. The burns were so bad he had to be treated at a local hospital.

In episode 9, physicists from Lunasonde arrived at the Ranch to conduct UAP and other phenomena above and below ground with low-frequency radio waves captured by a special balloon and equipment 70,000 feet above the triangle area. The scan will create a tomographic map of what lies below the ground. Tomography is imaging by sections or sectioning that uses any kind of penetrating wave.

The Team launched a rocket and mortar off a pickup bed above the mysterious triangle area where instruments fail and sometimes rockets vanish or a UAP appears. The first rocket exploded. But data was collected and analyzed from the tomographic map.

Caretakers at the Ranch Kandus Linde and Tom Lewis interviewed Tribal Fish & Game Ute Nation Officer Corey Reid. Reid takes them to the Ranch's south field where two horses were killed in a bizarre way years ago. The horses were cleaned out from the inside --no organs left and strange footprints around the carcasses of two 3-toed prints, 6" inches long. Reptilian aliens have been described as having 3 fingers and 3 toes with claws. Officer Corey Reid said he felt a negative presence in the area and did not like being there. The dead horses were in the same area as the dead deer and burnt post found in the previous episode.

Officer Corey Reid said he had taken photographs of the dead horses, filing a field report. Not long after Reid went back to find the photographs and report, but both had vanished as if someone didn't want the truth known.

A horse skeleton was discovered in the south field.

3-toed print of unknown creature.

Could the creature have been a reptilian being? Descriptions of reptilians resemble extinct dinosaurs that roamed Earth millions of years ago.

Again, the Skinwalker team returned and fired rockets into the triangle area using thermal cameras. The rocket reached 100 feet in the air. The mortar and rocket collide in the air as they are broadcasting a 1.6 gigahertz signal, the same frequency heard during previous experiments at the Ranch. The rocket flew into mortar which should not have happened.

The flare image revealed an oblong blob image in white above the triangle. White indicates something extremely hotter than the rest of the area. Suddenly an airplane appeared in the sky that wasn't transponding like it should. Any aircraft in the air should transpond their location. Unmarked military black helicopters and planes have been observed flying above the Ranch as if gathering data and observing the experiments.

Transponders exist in essentially all air vehicles (including, for example, not only airplanes, but helicopters, blimps, etc.), and some of those, especially in the military, operate in special modes that "regular" small airplanes do not have.

Cattle on the Ranch are shown on the thermal imagining as the blob image in the sky pulsed and changed temperatures.

Three days later Jeremiah Pate of Lunasonde joined a Zoom call with the Skinwalker Team. They discussed the analysis of the balloon data, and thought the balloon flight was flawless, but the electromagnetic levels kept jumping. At 10,000 feet above the Ranch the frequency changed--something seemed to be in the sky, invisible to the naked eye.

Here's the freaky part: there was a scan anomaly where a quarter of a second in time was lost as if it hit a "time shift" or portal. The team and Dr. Travis Taylor believed this was evidence of a dimensional portal where UAPs can appear and disappear in seconds.

Photo of silver orb that appeared on outdoor video traveling at an incredible speed, and photo on the right is Dr. Taylor's computer image of the silver orb.

Dimensional Portals

There are many areas across the world known to be energetic hotspots—from ancient megaliths to Ley Lines, these areas are often alleged to produce hyper-dimensional gateways. While scientists don't exactly know how to open a portal to another dimension, there is evidence the phenomenon could exist. And now it seems science may be catching on to the possibility.

Typically, portal areas have some type of electromagnetic significance and are located near large deposits of quartz or other minerals with piezoelectric properties. So, it came as less of a surprise when NASA announced in 2012 that the University of Iowa physicist Jack Scudder had evidence of portals created by the interaction between the Earth and the Sun's magnetospheres. These portals are extremely volatile and unpredictable, opening and closing in a matter of an instant. But Scudder found markers, called x-points or electron diffusion regions, which allowed NASA probes to locate and study them.

The Navajos, and the Utes, have believed for centuries that a portal exists in the Skinwalker Ranch area. The ancients believed there were doorways to other planes of existence. They identified particular places considered energetically anomalous, and in these areas, one finds either a succession of temples or a temple that has withstood the test of time.

If portals exist in the sky and on the ground, Puerta de Hayu Marca in Peru fits the description, located on the western banks of Lake Titicaca. Puerta de Hayu Marca translates to the Gate of the Gods. Reaching 23 feet in both height and width, Hayu Marca appears to be a doorway to nowhere carved into a rock face in a remote area known as the Valley of the Spirits or Stone Forest.

In a previous chapter, portals are believed to exist on other planets and what might appear to be a lifeless planet may hold life once the portal is entered. Imagine beings who hold such technology and traverse the Universe in a flash or as they say in Trekkie language, "Warped Speed."

The Secret of Skinwalker Ranch, Season 4

If things couldn't get stranger, they did in the History Channel's *Secret of Skinwalker Ranch*, episode 10. The drilling on top of the Mesa stopped suddenly when the driller hit something hard 25 feet down. In an earlier episode, an anomaly appeared in the thermal scanning into the Mesa. Previous drilling produced from the Mesa revealed a material that is used by NASA to protect the outside of their space missions.

The drill bit couldn't penetrate whatever was blocking it inside the Mesa. Experiments revealed what might be a dome-like structure inside the Mesa. The drilling on top was put on hold until next year's Season 5.

Native Americans believe that drumming produces certain frequencies that attract the Sky People from portals.

Astrophysicist Travis Taylor, team members Kaleb Bench and Thomas Winterton launched a rocket into the triangle area. Meanwhile, high-speed imaging systems specialist Burdette Anderson set up his photron cameras that shoot 2,000 images per second. The camera is usually used for slow motion analysis.

The launch of the rocket and the acoustic sound generated at that moment caught a UAP traveling across the sky unnoticed. It traveled across the sky in 1.2 seconds, 6 seconds after the launch. Travis calculated it was moving at 3,600 miles per hour without causing a wake or any atmospheric movement.

The craft was operating frictionless in the atmosphere, according to Travis, and compared their experiment to the 2004 U.S.S. Navy Nimitz pilots that captured a UAP on radar that seemed to have a force field around it.

What was the stimulus?

Later that evening principal investigator and chief scientist Erik Bard created higher and lower acoustic tones hoping to produce a certain frequency to activate something at the Ranch. Travis felt the ground resonate from the 192-hertz frequency. At the same time, a UAP appeared in the night sky above them, and a few minutes later, Erik replayed the 92 hertz, and another UAP appeared and vanished.

Suddenly, a UAP appeared in the night sky above them, and a few minutes later, Erik played the 192-hertz, and another UAP appeared and vanished.

Retired Navajo Nations Ranger John Dover told the team that Indigenous people in the area had used sound frequency to open up portals and had seen UAPs flying into the Mesa.

John Ballard and his Native American Blazing Bear drummers arrived at the Ranch from Oklahoma to participate in a frequency experiment. They represented several tribes throughout the country. Nothing happened during the day, so they returned at 8:00 pm that evening.

During the drumming ceremony, the thermal scanning showed areas above them heating up. When they stopped so did the heat signature on the scanner. The weird thing was the Indigenous drumming and singing produced the 192-hertz frequency like Erik Bard's acoustic experiment earlier.

After a few minutes, John Ballard and the drummers decided to stop abruptly after they heard shuffling footsteps and saw a dark figure moving near some large boulders near the Mesa. They left the Ranch, fearful something evil was awakened by their drumming and chanting.

On August 1, 2023, The Secret of Skinwalker Ranch final episode aired for Season 4. The entire team and owner Brandon Fugal met at his Salt Lake City office to review all the the experiments they had collected in 2022. At the end of the hour segment, the entire team and Fugal were astounded by Jeremiah Pate's revelation from the radar satellite system data of the Mesa and triangle area of the Ranch. Jeremiah is the owner and CEO of Lunasonde, Inc. and has conducted radar scans of the entire area of the Ranch. The scan sees up to 2 kilometers underground, essentially taking an MRI scan of the planet.

The map scan of the area revealed subsurface dots indicating deep tunnels from 10 meters to 20 meters (66' feet) under the Ranch near the Triangle area and on the Mesa side made of metal. Are the tunnels manmade or perhaps built by an alien species? Does the military know about them?

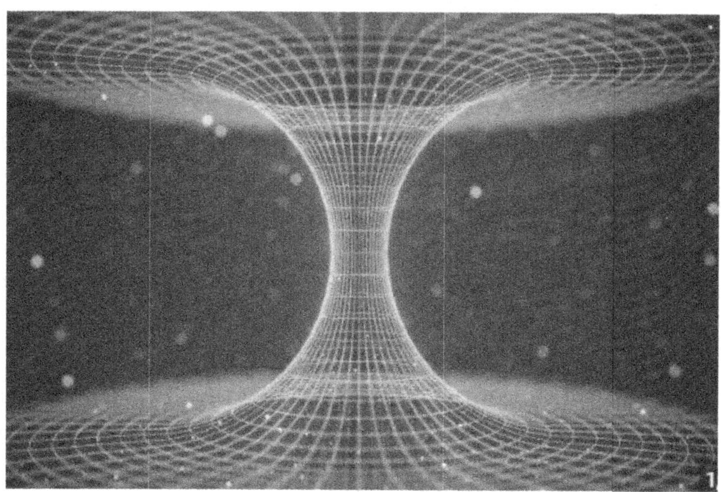

Transversable Wormhole

Dr. Travis Taylor theorizes that the large rocket fired into the Triangle in Episode 13, and vanished before their eyes, could indicate a Transverable Wormhole exists above and below that area. A wormhole is a hypothetical structure connecting disparate points in spacetime and is based on a special solution of the Einstein field equations. Such wormholes would allow UFOs or alien craft to move instantly across time and space. UAPs seen in the area appear and disappear instantly and orbs have been seen entering and exiting the Mesa as if they were flying into a bowl of Jello.

The Power of Resonance

Resonance and certain frequencies have been used throughout history. The Greek philosopher Pythagoras envisioned the universe as a harmonious whole and believed that everything in it emitted a sound or a "vibration."

The Old Testament Book of Genesis describes how the Universe was created by the "Word of God" which was probably a vibration, a sound that had enormous force and creation. The ancients believed that sound at certain frequencies could be used for creation or destruction. Today we know it's a scientific fact that certain frequencies can kill; even a soprano's high note can shatter a glass. The ancients also believed that it was possible to discover and apply the "word of God" for their own needs. Special words and music were used for invocations and the success achieved was thought to depend on the vibration and the pitch of the sound chosen because music, as well as words, can be related to numbers. It is believed the low vibrations are destructive and the higher vibrations are healing.

Vibration played a destructive role in the collapse of the 1940 Tacoma Narrows Bridge, a suspension bridge in the State of Washington that spanned the Tacoma Narrows Strait of Puget Sound between Tacoma and the Kitsap Peninsula. It opened to traffic on July 1, 1940, and collapsed into the Puget Sound on November 7 of the same year (strangely it happened on the 7th day, a power number). The date seemed to be connected to the event.

At the time of its construction and destruction, the bridge was the third longest suspension bridge in the world in terms of main span length, behind the Golden Gate Bridge and the George Washington Bridge. From the time the deck was built, it began to move vertically in windy conditions, which lead to construction workers dubbing it "Galloping Gertie." The motion was detected during the time it opened to the public, and several measures to stop it proved to be ineffective.

The bridge finally collapsed under 40-mile-per-hour (64km/h) wind conditions on the morning of November 7, 1940.

The bridge's collapse changed science and engineering in many ways. In physics textbooks, the event is presented as an example of elementary forced resonance, with the wind providing an external periodic frequency that matched the bridge's natural structural frequency. However, many believed the failure was due to aeroelastic flutter. The bridge's failure increased the research in the field of bridge aerodynamics-aeroelastic, the study of which has influenced the designs of all the world's great long-span bridges built since 1940.

The frequency number 7 was significant in the destruction of the walls of Jericho. According to the Book of Joshua, the Battle of Jericho was the first battle of the Israelites in their conquest of Canaan. According to Joshua 6:1-27, the walls of Jericho fell after Joshua's Israelite army marched around the city blowing their trumpets seven times on the 7th day.

"Now Jericho was shut up inside and outside because of the people of Israel. None went out, and none came in. And the Lord said to Joshua, "See, I have given Jericho into your hand, with its king and mighty men of valor. You shall march around the city, all the men of war going around the city once. Thus, shall you do it for six days? Seven priests shall bear seven trumpets of rams' horns before the ark. On the seventh day, you shall march around the city seven times, and the priests shall blow the trumpets. And when they make a long blast with the ram's horn when you hear the sound of the trumpet, then all the people shall shout with a great shout, and the wall of the city will fall down flat, and the people shall go up, everyone straight before him." ...

Is it possible mechanical resonance from marching around the city of Jericho caused the collapse of the walls? Acoustical resonance can produce the collapse of bridges and buildings as demonstrated in earthquakes and winds. Who knows what happened during Joshua's time, but we do know that sound is powerful stuff. We might also ask how Joshua obtained such an advanced weapon. Or was it pure luck that he instructed his people to march and sound their horns resulting in mechanical and acoustical resonance? I'd say he knew the properties of resonance through the Ark of the Covenant.

On July 5th, a 39-story office/shopping center building in Seoul, South Korea started to shake rapidly. For ten minutes vertical tremors violently rocked the building, causing an immediate evacuation of the premises. After the shaking subsided, engineers began a lengthy process to determine the cause of the incident. Eliminating earthquakes and windstorms, the culprit they landed on was bizarre, to say the least—an aerobics class of 23 people on a mid-level floor. Their Tae Bo workout was apparently twice as intense that day, making their fancy footwork synch up with the building's structural resonance.

More recently, London's Millennium Bridge was shut down in 2000 after a crowd created oscillating waves across the deck of the bridge. Like pushing a child on a swing at the correct moment so that her motion is amplified, resonance's effects are caused by the well-timed push of each wave. Push the swing at the right moment, and you could send the kid flying; amplify the vibrations in a building's structure enough, and you can cause it to collapse.

Nikola Tesla (1856-1943) once stated he could split the Earth in half through vibration or resonance, and his experiments may have proven he had that technology. He has been called "A Man out of Time" because of his futuristic experiments, inventions, and patents.

He discovered the power of resonance with an innocent experiment in 1898. Tesla attached a small vibrator to an iron column in his New York City laboratory and started it vibrating. At certain frequencies, specific pieces of equipment in the room began to jiggle. Change the frequency and the jiggle moved to another part of the room. Unfortunately, he hadn't accounted for the fact that the column ran downward into the foundation beneath the building. His vibrations were being transmitted all over Manhattan.

For Tesla, the first hint of trouble came when the walls and flood began to heave. He stopped the experiment just as the police crashed through his door. He had caused neighborhood windows to break, buildings to sway, and people to rush into the streets panicked. This was Tesla's oscillator which became known as a "reciprocating electricity generator".

Although Tesla was not the first to discover resonance, he was obsessed with it and created some of the most incredible demonstrations of it. Pythagoras experimented with it, and most likely there were others before Pythagoras. Tesla studied both mechanical and electrical versions. In the process, he was the first to create an artificial earthquake and numerous artificial lightning storms, and he could knock an entire power plant off-line in Colorado, and nearly caused the steel frame of a skyscraper under construction in Manhattan to collapse. He realized that the principles of resonance could be used to transmit and receive radio messages well before Marconi.

In fact, knowledgeable sources now credit Tesla as the inventor of the radio rather than Marconi. This includes what the Supreme Court ruled in 1943 that Tesla's radio patents had proceeded with all others including Marconi's patents.

Can you imagine what advanced aliens know about the universe and about resonance and how to power their spacecraft in a frictionless barrier that protects the occupants?

CHAPTER TWENTY

The Genetic Experiment

In the coming years, we will be shocked at the revelations about other inhabited planets in this and other solar systems. Many of them contain self-aware, sentient life forms advanced in technology and sciences perhaps thousands or millions of years ahead of us. Interplanetary travel has existed for what you would term eons of time. Much of the travel takes place in what you term "wormholes" or dimensional portals.

The visitors have different purposes for their visits by different representatives from various planets and are instrumental in altering human DNA. Some have a malevolent agenda, but there are benevolent beings of higher understanding that have been and are committed to helping humanity on Earth to cope with and transcend the future that is coming forth now. Many alterations have taken place.

In the beginning, they realized their mistake in creating a

being needed to do their work. They were slaves who became too aggressive. Because of this failed agenda, they simply shipped them off to a sparsely inhabited planet in a far-off corner of the galaxy where they would not be discovered, and then blamed for this failed experiment. To ensure this, all memory of this experience was erased, and no records were allowed to be taken by the altered humans on their trip to Earth. They were shipped in essence to a prison planet and left to either destroy each other or perhaps eventually work out their genetic imbalance through adaptation.

If you think that's impossible, think back to the colonization of the USA and Australia. The nation of England emptied its prisons in that process, doing the same thing with hopes of the same result. Did this act of enslavement interfere with the free will of this history of humanity? It did! Why then was it allowed to proceed? The offending planet made the acts by their free will choice, but through the law of attraction, so was the result of drawing to them a complimentary experience.

The trans-galactic shipment was not hidden from others. Other advanced beings were aware of the scenario and have over eons of time visited you. It became obvious that adaptation was not eliminating genetic error. Thus, a further experiment was begun.

The Bible refers to visitors finding the daughters of men fair and mating with them. This was to introduce another gene pool into abandoned humanity that would genetically alter future generations. They hoped the increased intelligence through the hybridization process might allow them to overcome the alteration by coming up with their own solution to the problem. Over time the introduction of extra gene pool additions has been made through carefully chosen genetic matching.

The overwhelming result has been the additional intelligence enhanced the aggressive tendencies within those not positively affected by the gene pool changes. They were reinforced with greater abilities to develop incredible weapons. They used the additional intelligence to organize to a high degree a hierarchy of power and control over the members of humanity on this planet that has evolved to a balanced genetic structure. Both negative results continue now.

Did the gene pool additions result in interfering with the planet in violation of the universal law of free will? None of this was done without it being cleared through ruling councils of galactic beings that focus creative energy and oversee the balance of the galaxy. There are benevolent beings that are part of the plan of creation that entails responsibilities of overseeing the galactic maintenance and expansion process.

Because genetic development was approved for this planet, other visitors have come to this plant as a source of gene pool improvement for their planetary inhabitants. This has been carried out with carefully selected individuals. Approval for this is given by these individuals beforehand through a certain process that involved the soul.

There is much knowledge that has been hidden from you and denied. But it is your right to know! Through manipulations by those still caught in the throes of genetic alteration that require them to pursue control to support their violent tendencies, you have been denied this information, even though it has been brought to Earth many times. Those in control of humanity live deep underground and on ocean bases. They work with some governments who desire their technology while turning humans over to them for genetic experiments.

Great teachers and those in the angelic realms have walked among us teaching us sacred knowledge, and because of being attacked and killed, have then come undetected to continue the gene pool experiments with selected recipients, educating them through clandestine meetings in attempts to bring you into awareness of who and what you are.

CONCLUSION

Something supernatural and deadly is happening in Alaska and around planet Earth. We can't deny that! A huge cover-up of mega proportions is taking place to hide the truth that extraterrestrials inhabit our planet.

The million-dollar question is what are they and why are they residing on and under our planet and in our deepest oceans? Abductees have been given many answers to their nature, biology, and reason for abducting and experimenting on humans, perhaps to confuse us. Has their advanced technology given them the ability to alter physical reality? The answer is yes when people have witnessed the so-called Watchers glide through doors and walls and other solid objects.

We are further confused by the variety of species seen. Some seem malevolent, some only want to observe us and others want to help us, or so they say. Who are they?

They are endless biological entities that travel our cosmos from multi-dimensions. They consider earthlings babies in the scheme of life. For some alien species, we are only a genetic experiment.

If a race, perhaps the reptilian race, who claims to dominate the Universe, exists beneath our deepest oceans and lakes, and underground, can we ever break away from their tenacious hold? Do they view us as guinea pigs for experimentation because they were instrumental in our accelerated evolution from the beginning? Some appear to want to help us; others appear ambivalent towards humans and consider us nothing more than specimens to be studied, while others show compassion for humans through healing. But there are those aliens who mock the pain of their captives. They are sadistic. Those are the cold-hearted reptilians.

Furthermore, do they fool us by using holographic images of angels and religious icons? I believe they do.

If our military and government collude with them for their technology, there must be some exchange that allows them to take us against our will. Star people are here whether we like it or not, and it does appear that their motives have evolved somewhat, but the main purposes of their visits have not changed. They are using humans for procreation.

Sometimes whistleblowers step forward with their tales of crash alien ships and dead gray aliens. The majority of humans are skeptical because they don't see any hard evidence of them and that's because their existence is TOP SECRET, and the military and governments are privy to this knowledge and hide the truth from humanity. Can you imagine if the President of the United States appeared on television one night to tell us that aliens are real and control our planet? Can you imagine the chaos, anger, and fear?

Certain cultures, like the Native Americans, have been in contact with certain Star People, and those relationships have not faded with time, but appear to be on the increase. Indian Reservations are in isolated areas in the West, and aliens can easily make contact with them as Dr. Ardy Sixkiller Clarke learned from her vast interviews with indigenous people from the United States to Central America.

Confusion and disbelief are our conceptions of what an alien should or shouldn't look like. We want them to look like us, but they don't. They appear to be a variety of species that look like the Cantina scene from *Star Wars* movie. Human abductees have described various sizes of gray aliens with big heads and huge eyes, the praying mantis aliens, the Ant Beings, the Nordic and Red-Headed humanoid aliens, the Blue Beings, the various Reptilians, and more.

In Dr. Ardy Sixkiller Clarke's book, *Sky People*, Native Americans described frightening reptilians five to nine feet tall with scaly greenish-brown skin, wide lipless mouths, and red eyes. Observers often report they have claws for their hands and feet. Reptilian aliens have been reported in Central America and during the Vietnam War. According to a Maya elder who encountered such a fearsome creature, its face resembled a lizard and its skin was a brownish-green, allowing it to blend in the jungle. The lizard creature stood ten feet high, yet it could jump into a tree thirty feet high.

Some reptilians are dark creatures who have nasty tempers. One Native American claimed he was blinded by a reptilian while serving in Vietnam. It hissed at him and sprayed venom at him.

Reptilians have proclaimed to their hostages that they are the master race of the Universe and control all other beings. Are they lying to us? We know that reptilians once dominated our planet and then were destroyed by a cataclysmic event 60 million years ago, or were they? Dinosaurs were intelligent, and perhaps they evolved through millions of years to become a superior race of beings who went underground.

If a benevolent energy we call God created all of us, as I believe it did, that includes the multitude of beings throughout the galaxies and dimensional realities. I do not doubt that they will need to evolve past their dark plans to a higher state of consciousness. Everything must evolve even if it takes billions of years in time as we know it.

My friend, MUFON investigator, and best-selling author Ann Druffel, often wondered if we could battle the malevolent alien entities. Ann's suggestions included prayer, anger, blocking them through mind control, and showing courage, but many others, including MUFON investigator Preston Dennett, found that certain aliens scoffed at humans who invoked the name of Jesus or God. One man was saved from a gray's mind control by repeating a prayer he learned as a child.

The prayer appeared to frustrate and confuse his abductors, and he was finally released from their hold.

In the *Mojave Incident* case, author Ron Felber used fictitious names for the couple abducted per their request. In his original book, *Searchers*, Felber revealed their actual names, Steve and Dawn Hess from Utah. They encountered three types of aliens in the Mojave Desert. A mother ship hovered above the desert and small UFO probes descended from it, yet our military did not see them or respond despite having numerous military bases throughout the Mojave including Area 51.

Many types of aliens have been reported by abductees through the years—blue people, the clone-like human-looking Elders in robes (Betty Andreasson Luca's description), Nordics, Red-headed human aliens, small grays, tall grays, various reptilian beings with scaled skin and some with wings, insect-like beings, alien-human hybrids with a large head and big eyes of different colors, and beings described only by Steve and Dawn Hess during their eight-hour abduction by three types of aliens in the Mojave Desert in 1989 (taken from *Mojave Incident* by Ron Felber). They described monitors who were grayish blue like electric images and the red-eyed monkey creatures. Lastly, there were the five-foot gray beings with raven-black eyes and long spindly appendages connected to an underdeveloped torso like a three-year-old child.

Before their ordeal ended in the desert, Steve and Dawn witnessed a white smoke, swirling from the left side of the sky. A beautiful being described as an 'angel'—radiant; and exquisite in appearance and nature, with a lucid robe moving as the woman floated towards them. In a voice that was soothing, comforting, and totally serene, she said, *"It's all right. I'm here now to protect you. Be at peace. It's almost over."*

The radiant being lifted in the air and moved away, and finally faded from view; making certain even to the end that they were safe from their torment.

Angels with aliens? Or aliens disguised as angels? Were Steve and Dawn shown dimensional holographic image of an angel by the abducting aliens to calm them during their hours of abduction and examinations?

I believe portals or stargates exist everywhere that allow travel instantly from any point in the universe. All planets have them, and our planet Earth is no exception to the rule. Places like Skinwalker Ranch in northeastern Utah, Bradshaw Ranch in Arizona, volcanoes, and undersea bases, are all portals for instant travel.

Even though such a theory sounds a bit like Star Trek, remember yesterday's science fiction is today's science.

Should scientists explore a simpler explanation for the visitors by using Occam's Razor which states that the simplest explanation is preferable to one that is more complex? If we were dealing with physical beings it might apply, but stories show we are not. Some may even be time travelers from the future.

Do we live in a ubiquitous computer simulation? The movie *The Matrix* did its part to popularize the notion of simulated realities. And the idea has deep roots in Western and Eastern philosophical traditions, from Plato's cave allegory to Zhuang Zhou's butterfly dream. More recently, Elon Musk gave further fuel to the concept that our reality is a simulation: "The odds that we are in a base reality is one in billions," he said at a 2016 conference. There's a discussion about time warps, wormholes, and the probability of multiple dimensions of reality proposed by new physics.

The alien entities revealed to Betty Andreasson Luca that their mode of travel is through the manipulation of space and time. In essence, they are not bound by the space-time constraints that restrict interstellar space travel by humans.

Raymond Fowler suggested in his book, *The Watcher II*, that either matter itself is eternal or it is created by an eternal consciousness (God?). And, what is matter?

Mojave Incident abductee Dawn Hess said this under hypnosis, "They always know where we are. They always know what we're thinking. They think they can do just anything they want!" When she was asked by the hypnotist if she had a sense as to who they are and where they come from, she said, "There are five galaxies. Theirs is the next closest. For all five galaxies to work together one day, they have to start and they're starting with us, so we'll be united galaxies. I know where the universe ends."

And then she gave this cryptic message, "Our universe ends where theirs begins. Our universe ends when all its matter stops mattering to us and starts mattering to them."

What a nebulous statement!

There are numerous extraterrestrials visiting Earth and perhaps some terrestrial beings that have existed here for eons. They can access dimensional portals on Earth and be anywhere in a flash. If a UAP flying over Skinwalker Ranch can fly at 3,600 mph in 1.2 seconds, just imagine how far more advanced they are than humans.

From the stories of humans abducted by different species, it appears there are both benevolent beings and malevolent ones including the reptilian race. Some view us with amusement, an experiment, some want to help us evolve and others want to only observe us and see if we destroy ourselves. At the moment, it appears we are on a destructive course.

Lizzies

I believe the lower lords or Lizzies that SunBow wrote about in his book are the reptilians. Why do you think humans are so fascinated with dinosaurs and reptiles? Because they are the story of our evolution on Earth.

Humans haven't always been human. The truth is we have not always been incarnated as human beings.

To some extent, the Lizzies have controlled this portal. They have used portals to create their deep underground bases worldwide and in deep caverns from which they operate. However, some deep ocean bases are inhabited by different beings than the Lizzies. The ancient civilization of Mesopotamia, between the Tigris and Euphrates rivers, was a space colony where a certain civilization was introduced. Kuwait sits at the mouth of this territory. This is a portal that involves the manipulation of the human population to serve the needs of others.

Within the Lizzie population, some are benevolent, and some are malevolent. The Lizzies can be compared to humans who are good and evil. You need to know this because the Lizzie reality is reentering and merging with your dimension. Part of your evolutionary leap in consciousness is not to go into love and light and eat ice cream sundaes every day. Humans must comprehend how complex reality is, how many different forms of reality and dimensions there are, and *how they are all you.* You must make peace with them and merge with them to create an implosion of the collection of your soul. In this way, you can return to Prime Creator.

In the years to come, you are going to be faced with many opportunities to judge many things and label them as bad. But, when you judge and label (this is happening everywhere), you will not experience and feel the new realities. Always remember that this is a free-will zone and that there is a Divine Plan, which is going to be the last plan, the last card to be played. You must all remember that this card is going to be an ace.

Creator alien gods take many forms, and they are not all Lizzies. There are creator gods who are insect-like, bird-like, and reptilians. Some beings came from space and worked with the energy of the birds in many different cultures. Look at the drawings found in ancient cultures of Egypt, South America, and North America and you will see signs of birds and reptiles. At one time the bird and reptile beings worked together, and at other times they fought. The story will get larger as you comprehend more and begin to remember your history.

Some of Earth's events are created by holographic technology that is so real you'd never know what is real and what is fake. They continue to experiment on humans and animals that often die from their experimentations. You do not realize that these situations are setups to get you to think or feel a certain way and to vibrate with a certain consciousness.

Suddenly mass consciousness is going to realize they will need to give up their delusion of reality like they gave up Santa Claus, the Easter Bunny, and the Tooth Fairy. The predominant energy on this planet siphons your belief systems according to its own will. It directs incredible flows of energy outward, and this energy is alive. You have been told that the mass consciousness of 8.0 billion humans on the planet is alive and creates reality. That much energy is alive on Earth.

Because this is a free-will universe, all forms of life are allowed here. You have no idea the multitude of life forms that co-exist around and within your planet. If an energy attempts to frighten you, manipulate you, or control you, it is not an energy that would be in your highest interest to work with, yet governments have colluded with the dark reptilians to gain some of their technology. Not all UFOs or UAPs are extraterrestrial. Some are human made by a division of the military classified as top secret.

Just because space beings like the Lizzies have great scientific knowledge doesn't mean they are spiritually evolved. That's what you must learn to discern. We want you to realize that those space gods on and around your planet that you dub "bad guys" with whom your government forces have made deals—are dealing with the same issues that you are. They are beings who reflect our beliefs and then return those beliefs to you. They have been accused of heinous behavior, performing mutilations, and abductions upon the human species, and this is true.

They are so enveloped in their own power that they fight amongst themselves. The creator gods are coming back to raid you again because they feed on fear. They know there is "system busting" happening worldwide through humans, so they are creating more havoc and fear to fight again for this territory. The truth is they are losing control of the planet.

These beings act as a mirror to show you your own world—what you acquiesce to and what you acquiesce to let your leaders do all over the world. How is your acquiescence to the government and media, and the way you are used any different from a cow who is mutilated by an extraterrestrial? What the Lizzies and other space beings do here is nothing different from what our species does.

Millions and millions of you have been abducted without any recall of the incident, and some of you know something is coming but you don't know what. Some beings play on both teams because they are double agents.

They have invaded the underworld where they conduct in secret their most detrimental and disruptive experiments for the evolution and balance of Earth, including magnet and genetic manipulations. They can control Earth's weather and create earthquakes anywhere on the planet.

You feel discomfort from beings of the reptilian type, but there are also insect-looking beings that have evolved over millions of years. Their technology makes human technology look like tinker toys. Earth is going through great turmoil because the gods are returning. As you learn to hold the frequencies coming from the creative cosmic rays, you will be prepared to meet these gods, not in secret but openly. Some of these remain hidden underground, deep within the oceans, and some of them walk your streets and participate in your sciences, your government, and your workplaces. Some have agendas and some are here to observe, and some are here to learn and evolve. Some do not have the highest of intentions for humanity.

Again, there are many lies, and deceptions put out by the lower gods through your governments. They want to be seen as the Star Elders and usurp the title of Earth Watchers while they have fallen from their duty to become Nephilim, (Nephilim, in the Hebrew Bible, are a group of mysterious beings or people of unusually large size and strength who lived both before and after the Flood.) The Nephilim are referenced in Genesis and Numbers and are possibly referred to in Ezekiel due to pride, arrogance, greed for power, and selfishness. They want to be seen as saviors and gods, and carry on their agenda for global control, through a centralized tyranny of their own, so they try to masquerade as the Council of Star Elders.

The collective soul of human beings has recognized increasingly the reality of their enslavement but tries to ignore it. But the human soul must act and change its ways to free itself from this age-old bondage. This is the last opportunity humans can grasp to end slavery and reconnect with the Cosmic Order, before the lower lords apply the next phase of their control agenda, which they are already mirroring to you, and modify once more your genetics by turning your species into biosynthetic cyborgs and artificial entities controlled by their technology. Already controlled hybrids cyborgs walk your cities. Most of them creating mayhem have no idea they are being controlled like pawns on a chessboard by reptilian beings. Have you wondered why your cities are falling apart?

Humans may think there are still years to go before being faced with this artificial recoding, but it is already taking place. The situation that our ancestors faced in the downfall of Atlantis is being replayed today, but on a much grander scale, that will cause unrepairable damage to your genetics, evolution, and destiny. If it is not stopped it could mean the soul evolution cosmic experiment will come to an abrupt halt with global destruction and mass extinction similar to the demise of Atlantis.

The soul of Mother Earth, although compassionate, is asking for the end of your enslavement and destruction and may speed up the purification process that has been engaged through the actions and behaviors of the lower lords who have been controlling you. However, higher cosmic forces and spiritual entities are watching and may intervene and transform the course of events.

It is your responsibility and duty to make sure that the ancient spiritual knowledge of your soul's evolutionary process remains alive and is passed on to the generations of the future so that they can remember the long road their ancestors have traveled. We don't know how far the agenda of the lower reptilian lords can be taken before reaching the breaking point that will upset the forces maintaining the balance of Earth, which could bring about another mass extinction level event. Earth is out of balance because of humans and the dark reptilians, and Earth is a sentient being that feels us and our emotions.

At this point, many dark agendas are lowering your vibration rate—5G, CERN experiments, the reptilians and their experiments, and our secret military and their heinous experiments on humanity. There are those in secret societies and the military who believe because they work with the Lizzies that they are protected, but the Lizzies are beholding to no one except themselves.

Our world could turn into a *Mad Max* scenario where everything is chaotic, and humans are on the run and hiding. Future generations must stay aligned with the Divine Law that will turn the planned events into one of Peace and Cosmic Order. There is no hope for a better world if humans keep supporting and serving the system of the Lizzies.

You must deprive the lower lords of their power and withdraw your support in all forms to their enslaving systems, recover the sovereignty of your Soul, and redesign your ways of self-governance through your spiritual circles that are aligned with the Divine and Higher Purpose of the Cosmos. Once the Lizzies are uncovered and revealed to the world, they will shrivel because they will discover they can no longer live on your energy. In the meantime, higher-evolved beings are selecting ambassadors to carry the message to those who are open to saving themselves and the planet. Many of you will become conduits through dreams, apparitions, whispers, and inspirations.

There is a probability that if energy runs amok there could be hundreds and thousands of years of dictatorship in this universal system. Who will you call to save you—Luke Skywalker? When you finally awaken with ancient eyes you will be able to open up to your personal history and connect with planetary history, the galactic history, and the universal history. Then you will see who your gods are.

Just because space beings like the Lizzies have great scientific knowledge doesn't mean they are spiritually evolved. That's what you must learn to discern. We want you to realize that those space gods on and around your planet that you dub "bad guys" with whom your government forces have made deals—are dealing with the same issues that you are. They are beings who reflect your beliefs and this returns to you. They have been accused of heinous behavior, performing mutilations, and abduction upon the human species, and this is true.

These beings act as a mirror to show you your own world—what you acquiesce to and what you acquiesce to let your leaders do all over the world. How is your acquiescence to the government and media, and the way you are used any different from a cow who is mutilated by an extraterrestrial? What the Lizzies and other space beings do here is nothing different from what your species does. The masses, as you have probably noticed, allow leaders to do as they wish in their name because the masses do not rise up and say, "Hey, I do not approve of this!" There is great complacency on Earth. The consciousness on this planet is, "You do it for me. I don't want to be responsible. You become my government official. You become my teacher. You become my boss. You do not want the truth, so you say, *Someone tells me what to do*.

Many of you who know the truth will be shocked and appalled at the stupidity and ideological worship that the rest of the human race will show toward certain space beings who pass themselves off as your creators even though they do not resemble the human species. They will be able to do extraordinary feats of science and will share their technologies. They will cure certain diseases as they have done in the past that they helped create in the first place by teaching germ warfare to human scientists.

Those of you who understand the enormity of the situation will be disgusted by society and you will want to retreat. Do you understand the new gods are lizard "Lizzies?" When you pull back the curtain you will see the wizard is a reptilian. You think that's crazy—hold onto your seats, because you have no idea what is coming. If you knew what was coming, you would have scattered a long time ago.

POSTSCRIPT

Alaska's Missing Indigenous People

I first became aware of hundreds of missing indigenous women in *Alaska Daily,* an American drama television series created by Tom McCarthy for ABC, starring Hilary Swank as a journalist seeking a fresh start in Anchorage, Alaska. It premiered on October 6, 2022.

Many of *Alaska Daily's* storylines are inspired by real events chronicled in "Lawless: Sexual Violence in Alaska," a Pulitzer Prize-winning series of articles by Kyle Hopkins, a reporter for the Anchorage Daily News.

For decades, Native American and Alaska Native communities have struggled with high rates of assault, abduction, and murder of women. Community advocates describe the crisis as a legacy of generations of government policies of forced removal, land seizures, and violence inflicted on Native peoples.

A 2016 study by the National Institute of Justice (NIJ) found that more than four in five American Indian and Alaska Native women (84.3 percent) have experienced violence in their lifetime, including 56.1 percent who have experienced sexual violence.

- In the year leading up to the study, 39.8 percent of American Indian and Alaska Native women had experienced violence, including 14.4 percent who had experienced sexual violence.

- Overall, more than 1.5 million American Indian and Alaska Native women have experienced violence in their lifetime.

Victimization Rates

Native American and Alaska Native rates of murder, rape, and violent crime are all higher than the national average. When looking at missing and murdered cases, data shows that Native American and Alaska Native women make up a significant portion of missing and murdered individuals.

- According to the Centers for Disease Control and Prevention, the murder rate is ten times higher than the national average for women living on reservations, and the third leading cause of death for Native women. Additionally, this group was significantly more likely to experience rape in their lifetimes compared to other women.

- According to a 2008 report titled Violence Against American Indian and Alaska Native Women and the Criminal Justice Response: What is Known national rates of homicide victimization against American Indian and Alaska Native women are second to those of their African American counterparts.
- Like other women, American Indian and Alaska Native women are more likely to be killed by their intimate partners compared to other offenders.

The NIJ study also found that American Indian and Alaska Native men, too, have high victimization rates.

- More than four in five American Indian and Alaska Native men (81.6 percent) have experienced violence in their lifetime. And, overall, more than 1.4 million American Indian and Alaska Native men have experienced violence in their lifetime.

Human Trafficking

In September 2017, the Government Accountability Office (GAO) released a report titled "Human Trafficking: Investigations in Indian Country or Involving Native Americans and Actions Needed to Better Report on Victims Served." GAO surveyed tribal and major city law enforcement agencies and victim service providers on human trafficking investigations, victim services, and barriers to identifying and serving Native victims.

Twenty-seven of the 132 tribal law enforcement agencies that responded to the survey reported initiating investigations involving human trafficking from 2014 to 2016 and six of 61 major city law enforcement agencies reported initiating human trafficking investigations that involved at least one Native victim during the same period. Survey respondents identified a lack of training on identifying and responding appropriately to victims, victim shame and reluctance to come forward, and a lack of service provider resources as barriers to investigating cases and serving victims.

Need for Focused Data

While these rates are staggering, research data shows that national averages hide the extremely high rates of murder against American Indian and Alaska Native women present in some counties comprised primarily of tribal lands. According to the National Institute of Justice Centers for Disease Control and Prevention 2008, the National Violence Against Women

Survey (NVAWS), less than half of violent victimizations against women are ever reported to the police.

According to the National Crime Information Center, in 2016, there were 5,712 reports of missing American Indian and Alaska Native women and girls, through the US Department of Justice's federal missing persons database, but the national information clearinghouse and resource center for missing, unidentified, and unclaimed person cases across the United States, called the National Missing and Unidentified Persons System (NamUs) only logged 116 of those cases.

- While it is estimated that rates of violence on reservations can be up to ten times higher than national averages, research is missing on rates of murder violence among American Indian and Alaska Native women living in urban areas. An NIJ-funded study from 2008 found that the rates of violence on reservations are much higher than the national average. However, according to the Urban Indian Health Institute, no research has been done on the rates of such violence among American Indian and Alaska Native women living in urban areas even though approximately 71 percent of American Indian and Alaska Natives live in urban areas.

- Moreover, reports indicate that there is no reliable count of how many Native women go missing or are killed each year. Researchers have found that women are often misclassified as Hispanic or Asian or other racial categories on missing-person forms and that thousands have been left off federal missing-persons.

Need for Investigative Resources

Statistics show us that approximately 1,500 American Indian and Alaska Native missing persons have been entered into the National Crime Information Center (NCIC) throughout the U.S. and approximately 2,700 cases of Murder and

Nonnegligent Homicide Offenses have been reported to the Federal Government's Uniform Crime Reporting (UCR) Program. In total, BIA estimates there are approximately 4,200 missing and murder cases that have gone unsolved.

These investigations remain unsolved often due to a lack of investigative resources available to identify new information from witness testimony, re-examine new or retained material evidence, as well as reviewing fresh activities of suspects. Source: U.S. Department of Interior Indian Affairs

---

Should we count the 16,000 plus humans who have vanished in Alaska without a trace through the years as part of the indigenous men, women, and children who have been murdered or victims of human trafficking? That's a definite yes, but that still doesn't explain over 11,000 other disappearances in Alaska.

BIBLIOGRAPHY

Berlitz, Charles, *The Dragon's Triangle*, 1989.

Blatty, William Peter, *The Exorcist,* Harper and Rows, New York, NY, 1971.

Clarke, Ardy Sixkiller, *Space Age Indians: Their encounters with the Blue Men, Reptilians, and Other Star People,* Anomalist Books, San Antonio, TX, 2019. *Sky People*, New Page Books, Pompton Plains, NJ, 2015.

Cohens, Daniel, *Curses, Hexes and Spells*, 1974.

Dennett, Preston, The Healing Power of UFOs: 300 True Accounts of People Healed by Extraterrestrials, 2019, Blue Giant Books.

Dihle, Bjorn, *Haunted Inside Passage,* Alaska Northwest Books, Portland, Oregon, 2017.

Druffel, Ann, *The Tujunga Canyon Contacts,* Prentice-Hall, 1980 and *How to Defend Yourself Against Alien Abduction*, 1998, Three Rivers Press, New York, New York 10022.

Felber, Ron, *Mojave Incident*, Barricade Books, 2015, Fort Lee, New Jersey

Fowler, Raymond, *The Andreasson Affair, Englewood: Prentice Hall, 1982, The Watchers, New York: Bantam Books, 1990, The Watchers II, Newberg, Oregon: Wildflower Press, 1995, UFO Testament.*

Gernon, Bruce, *Beyond the Bermuda Triangle,* The Career Press, Wayne, New Jersey, 2017.

Mayor, Adrienne, *Fossil Legends of the First Americans,* Princeton University Press, Reprint 2023.

Michel, Aime, *Flying Saucers and the Straight Line Mystery,* 1958, no longer available.

Paulides, David, *Missing 411 (several editions) Create Space. 2012.*

SunBow, *The Sasquatch Message to Humanity, Comanche Spirit Publishing, 2016.*

ABOUT THE AUTHOR

Betsey Lewis began investigating UFOs and mysterious cattle mutilations in the 1970s. At eight months old, she and her parents had a UFO encounter on a farming road in Northwestern Idaho late one night as they traveled to Southern Idaho. Years later, a family member recalled her parents' incident when a roar engulfed the car. The roar and the two hours of missing time could not be explained until 1983 when renowned MUFON investigator Ann Druffel used hypnosis on Betsey and her mother. They both revealed that on that frightening night they had been abducted by small gray aliens with huge black eyes and returned them to their car two hours later.

At age seven, Betsey witnessed a UFO while walking home from her elementary school in Twin Falls, Idaho. Shortly after the event, she was shown catastrophic Earth changes in recurring dreams that are now taking place worldwide.

Betsey has investigated alien stories, UFOs sightings, ancient archaeological sites in Louisiana, and Native American petroglyph sites throughout the Northwest. She conducted field investigations into the bizarre cattle mutilations throughout the Northwest during the late 1970s and early 1980s and collaborated with Tom Adams, author of the *Stigmata Report* and renowned cattle mutilation investigator.

Betsey's guest interviews include Coast-to-Coast AM, Ground Zero with Clyde Lewis, Ktalk's Fringe Radio, Fade to Black, WGSO AM in New Orleans, and other well-known shows. She was a keynote speaker at the Alamo/Las Vegas UFO Conference in 2013 and a keynote speaker at the UFO Conference in Albuquerque, New Mexico in 2017. She has authored seventeen non-fiction Amazon books and three fictional children's books available on Amazon.

To learn more about Betsey, her books, upcoming events, and her daily Earth News blog visit **www.betseylewis.com**

Made in the USA
Monee, IL
10 November 2023

46201997R00118